THE *NEW* MALAYSIAN COOKBOOK

THE *NEW* MALAYSIAN COOKBOOK

NOR ZAILINA NORDIN
A T.V. personality in cooking and a prominent judge
in cooking competitions. Also a recipe writer to popular magazines:
'Her World', 'Keluarga', 'Jelita', 'Ibu'.

FATIHAH SEOW BOON HOR
A cook with 48 years experience and who has cooked for royalty:
His Highness the Sultan of Selangor & His Highness the Sultan of Pahang.
Conducts regular cooking classes.

Food Editor **Faudziah Bedu, BA (Hons)**
Project Coordinator **Rani Ranjit Kaur**

Photography **Daniel T.S. Kon**

CONTENTS

PRESTON CORPORATION

MALAYSIA (7332-V)
18 Jalan 19/3
46300 Petaling Jaya
Selangor Darul Ehsan
Malaysia
Tel: 03-79563734/5
Fax: 03-79573607
Email: presco@po.jaring.my

SINGAPORE
9 Irving Place
Singapore 369550
Tel: 2826721 & 2826875
Fax: 2853453
Email: prestonsg@pacific.net.sg

OVERSEAS DISTRIBUTION RIGHTS
All enquiries to
Publishing Manager
e-mail: presco@po.jaring.my
        prestonsg.pacific.net.sg

© Preston Corporation Sdn Bhd

ISBN 983-158-151-2

First published 2001

CHICKEN

Fried Lemon Chicken **16**
Maltose Chicken Wings **17**
Spicy Fried Chicken **23**
Ayam Golek (Stuffed Chicken) **26**
Soto Ayam **32**
Ayam Kurma **33**
Opor Ayam **44**
Tandoori Chicken **66**
Serunding Ayam (Chicken Floss) **79**
Fried *Pandan* Chicken **89**
Ayam Masak Merah **102**
Braised Chicken with Mushrooms **108**
Chicken *Siew Pau* **110**
Ayam Percik **115**
Chicken Satay **116**
Chicken with Young Ginger **126**
Chicken Kampung-Style **134**
Dry Chicken Curry **136**
Chicken *Kut Teh* **145**
Rendang Ayam **155**
Ayam Masak Kicap (Chicken with Soya Sauce) **157**
Cencaluk-Flavoured Chicken **162**

MEAT

Beef Curry **18**
Mutton Kurma **19**
Daging Masak Merah Ala Thai **34**
Bergedel Daging (Meat Patties) **35**
Serunding Daging (Beef Floss) **42**
Sup Tulang (Ox Bone Soup) **43**
Kambing Keema (Mutton Keema) **46**
Daging Bakar Cecah Air Asam **80**
Telur Bungkus Daging (Stuffed Eggs) **90**
Mutton Soup **129**
Dendeng Daging **138**
Rendang Tok **139**

SEAFOOD

Ketam Asam Pedas (Hot and Sour Crabs) **15**
Prawn Sambal with Petai **30**
Sweet and Sour Fish **31**
Spicy Fried Prawns **47**
Fish Curry **51**
Ikan Patin Masak Tempoyak **56**

Sweet and Sour Fish Soup **65**

Fish Head Curry **67**

Spicy Fried Squids **68**

Fried Cuttlefish with Mixed Vegetables **76**

Ketam Masak Lemak Cili Padi **82**

Squids in Spicy Santan **94**

Stuffed Squids **106**

Stuffed Fried *Cencaru* **119**

Grilled Fish **121**

Ikan Pari Masak Asam Pedas **124**

Masala Machi **133**

Chaozhou Steamed Fish **149**

Ketam Masak Pedas (Hot and Spicy Crabs) **156**

Mixed Tom Yam **158**

Pindang Serani **159**

Yong Tow Foo **161**

Lala Masak Pedas (Hot and Spicy Clams) **172**

Buttered-Flavoured Prawns **174**

VEGETABLES

Stir-fried Mixed Vegetables **20**

Bhujia Ladies' Fingers **21**

Pecal **36**

Kai Lan with Beef **37**

Paceri Nanas **48**

Dhal Curry **49**

Fried *Choy Tam* **50**

Kerabu Pucuk Paku **63**

French Beans with Liver **71**

Asparagus with Prawns **72**

Kerabu Tauge **81**

Bergedel Sayur (Vegetable Patties) **88**

Mixed Fried *Sambal* **93**

Vegetable Soup **97**

Acar Sayur Campur (Pickled Mixed Vegetables) **109**

Szechuan Tofu **118**

Malay-style Rojak **120**

Pucuk Ubi Masak Tempoyak **125**

Yam in Assam Gravy **127**

Kubis Masak Lemak (Cabbage in Coconut Milk) **140**

Fried *Kangkung* with *Belacan* **141**

Sayur Cekur Berkeledek **146**

Ulam dengan Cicah (Vegetables with Dip) **147**

Stuffed Bean Curd **160**

Fried Four Angled-Beans **164**

RICE & BREAD

Tomato Rice **22**

Claypot Rice **24**

Nasi Minyak **38**

Hailam Chicken Rice **39**

Pulut Kuning (Yellow Glutinous Rice) **62**

Nyonya Fried Rice **64**

Nasi Beriani Hujan Panas (Colourful Rice) **70**

Chapati **73**

Nasi Lemak with Anchovy Sambal **77**

Yang Zhou Fried Rice **78**

Nasi Kerabu **83**

Chang Parcels **95**

Lemang **98**

Thosai **105**

Nasi Dagang - Gulai Ikan Tongkol **112**

Lontong **113**

Roti Canai **117**

Ketupat (Compressed Rice in Coconut Leaves) **135**

Nasi Ulam **137**

Putu Mayam (String-Hoppers) **142**

Murtabak **150**

Puri **169**

NOODLES

Johor Laksa **25**

Mee Siam **52**

Indian Fried Mee **53**

Mee Jawa **69**

Prawn Mee **96**

Curry Mee **99**

Mee Bandung **101**

Laksam **114**

Penang Fried *Kuey Teow* **144**

Fish Head Meehoon Soup **148**

Assam Laksa **152**

CONTENTS

KUIH & OTHERS

Kuih Bahulu **28**

Samosas **40**

Yau Cha Kwai **45**

Kuih Ketayap **54**

Lepat Pisang **55**

Otak-otak **58**

Kuih Talam **60**

Kuih Koci **74**

Kuih Kosui **84**

Kuih Seri Muka **85**

Kuih Lapis **103**

Kuih Kole Kacang **104**

Buah Melaka **122**

Curry Puffs **128**

Masala Vadei **130**

Pakoras **132**

Pulut Inti (Glutinous Rice with Coconut) **143**

Dodol **153**

Chinese Radish Cake **154**

Yam Cake **163**

Popia (Spring Rolls) **165**

Muruku **166**

Kuih Tepung Pelita **168**

Kuih Ang Koo **173**

DESSERTS

Cendol **29**

Loh Hon Kor **57**

Tau Foo Fa **61**

Seaweed Jelly **86**

Bubur Cha Cha **87**

Ice Cream Pudding **92**

Bubur Kacang Hijau (Green Mung Beans Porridge) **100**

Pengat Pisang (Banana Porridge) **111**

Leng Chee Kang **131**

Jala Emas **170**

Glossary of Ingredients **6**

Index **175**

GLOSSARY OF INGREDIENTS

Spring Onions

Galangal

Young Ginger

Ginger

Local Limes

Limes

Lime Leaves / Kaffir
Lime Leaves

Mint Leaves

Coriander
Leaves

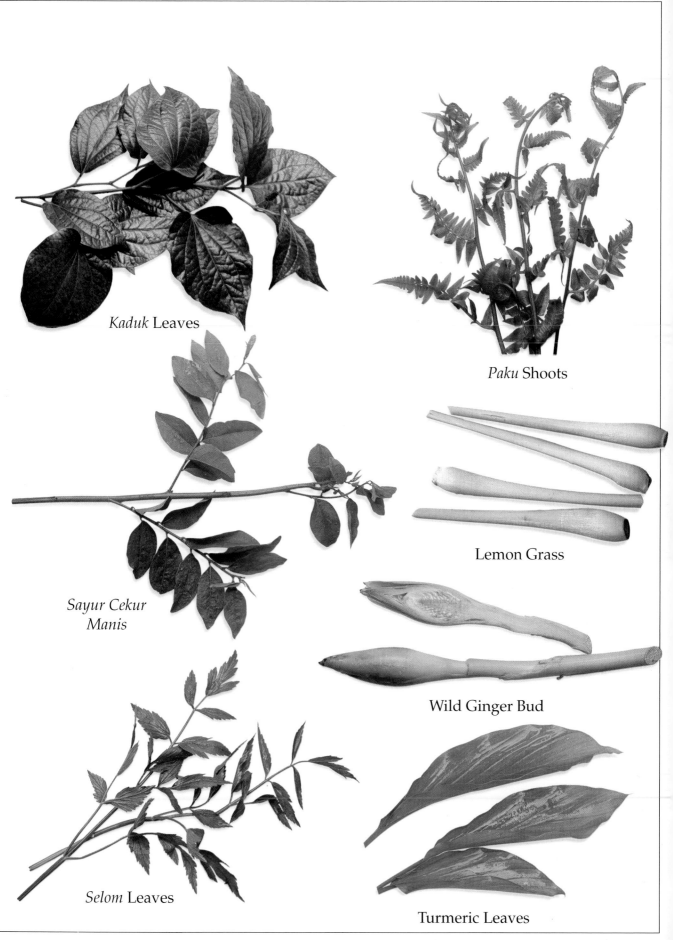

Kaduk Leaves

Paku Shoots

Sayur Cekur Manis

Lemon Grass

Wild Ginger Bud

Selom Leaves

Turmeric Leaves

GLOSSARY OF INGREDIENTS

Bird's Eye
Chillies
(*Cili Padi*)

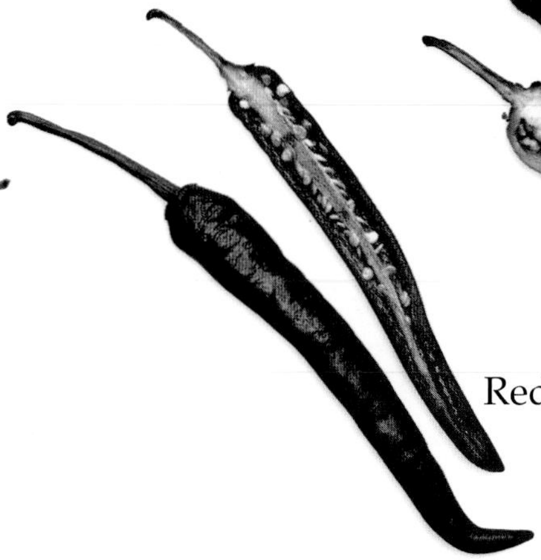

Green Chillies

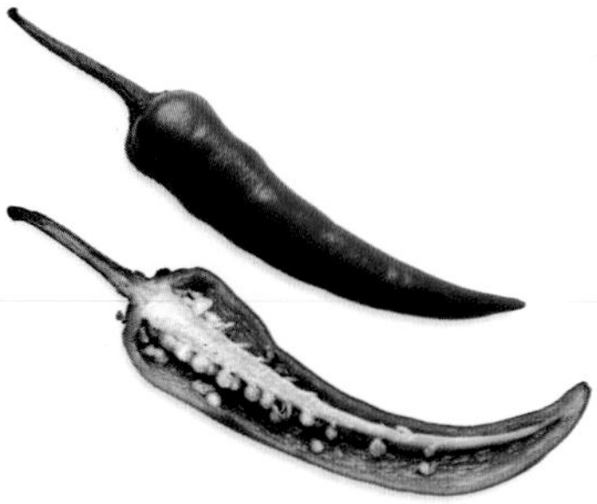

Red Chillies

Chinese Parsley

Turmeric

Tapioca Shoots

Screwpine Leaves/
(*Daun Pandan*)

Four-angled Beans

Yam Stalks

Beancurd

Beansprouts

Chives

Daun Ulam
Raja

Fermented
Beancurd
(*Tempe*)

Curry Leaves

Petai

GLOSSARY OF INGREDIENTS

Red Dates

Tapioca Starch

Cardamom

Fennel

Green (mung)
Beans

Split Black
Peas

Green Bean
Flour

White Sesame

Coriander

Star Anise

Cloves

Mustard Seeds

Black Peppercorns

Nutmeg

Chilli Powder

Curry Powder

Rice Flour

Chickpea Flour

Turmeric Powder

Wheat Flour /Plain Flour

Kei Chi

Potato Starch

Yellow Dhal

Red Beans

Black Glutinous Rice

Pak Kor (Gingko Nuts)

Cornflour

Choy Po (Dried Radish)

GLOSSARY OF INGREDIENTS

Palm Sugar

Tamarind Paste/
Asam

Brown Sugar

Kerisik (Ground Crispy
Fried Coconut)

Papadam

Sup Bunjut (Dry
Spices In Muslin)

Tong Fan (Glass Noodles)

Rock Sugar

Fucuk (Dried Bean Curd Sheets)

Roasted Seaweed

Dried Shrimp Paste

Agar-agar

Tamarind Skin (Dried)

Dried Oyster

5-spice Powder

Kam Cham (Dried Lily Buds)

Cinnamon Sticks

GLOSSARY OF INGREDIENTS

Wan Yee (Black Cloud
Ear Fungus)

Mok Yee (Wood Ear
Fungus)

Dried Mushrooms

Purple Laver Seaweed

Fatt Choy (Hair Vegetable)

Sheet Yee (White Woods
Ear Fungus)

Dried Chillies

KETAM ASAM PEDAS *(Hot and Sour Crabs)*

Serves 4

1 kg. crabs (halved)
2 stalks lemon grass/serai
   (bruised)
2 slices dried assam
1 turmeric leaf/daun kunyit
   (shredded)
sufficient water (to cover crabs)
salt & sugar to taste

BLENDED INGREDIENTS
6 shallots
3 cloves garlic
1 cm. turmeric/kunyit
½ cm. ginger
½ cm. galangal/lengkuas
1 cm. dried shrimp paste/belacan
8-10 dried chillies (soaked till soft)

1 Mix the blended ingredients, lemon grass, dried assam, turmeric leaf and water in a pot. Bring to the boil.

2 Put in the crabs and adjust the salt and sugar to taste.

3 Stir occasionally till mixture is boiling and crabs are well-cooked.

4 Remove from heat. Dish up onto a serving platter.

5 Serve crabs hot with boiled white rice or fresh bread.

FRIED LEMON CHICKEN

Serves 4

1 whole chicken
oil for frying

MARINADE INGREDIENTS
a pinch of five spice powder
1 egg
1 teaspoon chicken stock
granules
2 tablespoons custard powder

SAUCE INGREDIENTS
1 lemon (juice extracted)
1 tablespoon sour plum sauce
1 tablespoon sugar
a pinch of ⎱ **mixed**
cornflour ⎰ **thoroughly**
a little water
250 ml water

1 Clean the chicken and pat dry with a cloth. Split the breast (do not cut through). Remove bones from the thighs and wings.

2 Coat the five spice powder, egg and chicken stock granules all over chicken. Then, coat chicken with custard powder. Put aside for 30 minutes.

3 Heat oil and fry the chicken over low heat until golden.

Remove and drain. Leave to cool. Cut fried chicken into small pieces and set aside.

4 To prepare sauce: Leave a small amount of oil in the wok. Add in the sauce ingredients and simmer until sauce thickens.

5 Dish out sauce and pour onto a serving plate. Arrange the chicken pieces on top and serve hot.

MALTOSE CHICKEN WINGS

Serves 4

1 kg chicken wings
1 lemon (juice extracted)
sufficient water
oil for frying

MARINADE INGREDIENTS
1 teaspoon shallots ⎱ **chopped**
1 teaspoon garlic ⎰
a pinch of chilli powder
a pinch of salt
1 tablespoon ginger juice
3 tablespoons maltose (melted)

1 Boil water and add lemon juice. Leave to boil.

2 Add in chicken wings. Remove when the skin has shrunk. Drain chicken wings.

3 Marinade chicken wings with marinade ingredients for 30 minutes.

4 Heat oil. Fry chicken wings over low heat until golden brown or cooked.

5 Remove from heat and drain well. Serve hot on a serving plate.

Beef Curry

Serves 6

1 kg. beef (cut into bite-sized pieces)
60 ml. oil
5 cm. cinnamon stick ⎫
4 cloves ⎪
1 star anise ⎬ dry spices
3 cardamoms ⎭
1 stalk curry leaf/daun kari
1 tablespoon *asam jawa* ⎫ mixed &
50 ml. water ⎭ strained
1.2 *l* coconut milk (from 1 coconut)
sufficient water
3 medium potatoes (peeled & quartered)
salt & sugar to taste

BLENDED INGREDIENTS
1 large onion
6 shallots
4 cloves garlic
4 cm. ginger

BLENDED SPICES
3 tablespoons meat curry powder ⎫
1 tablespoon chilli powder ⎪
2 teaspoons coriander ⎬ mixed with water to a paste
powder ⎪
2 teaspoons fennel powder ⎪
1 teaspoon turmeric powder ⎭

1 Sauté the dry spices and curry leaves in hot oil for 1-2 minutes.

2 Mix in the blended ingredients; stir till fragrant.

3 Add in blended spices paste. As soon as the oil floats, add in the beef pieces.

4 Stir for a further 4-5 minutes or until the water has dried up.

5 Gradually pour in *asam jawa* juice and coconut milk. Adjust seasoning.

6 Stir curry occasionally till boiling and the meat is almost tender. Add water if necessary.

7 When beef pieces are tender, mix in potatoes.

8 Cook until the potatoes are soft. Remove and serve curry hot with boiled white rice.

MUTTON KURMA

Serves 6

- 1 kg. mutton (diced into 25 pieces)
- 100 g. kurma powder
- 1 tablespoon lime juice
- 80 ml. oil
- 10 shallots
- 2 cloves garlic } thinly sliced
- 6 cardamoms
- 1 star anise
- 5 cm. cinnamon stick } dry spices
- 6 cloves
- 800 ml. thin coconut milk
- 200 ml. thick coconut milk } from 1½ coconuts
- 3 potatoes (peeled & quartered)
- 1 slice dried assam
- 2 tomatoes
- 1 large onion } quartered
- 4 red chillies
- 3 green chillies } halved lengthwise; do not split
- 4 candlenuts
- 2 tablespoons poppy seeds } finely pounded
- salt & sugar to taste

1 Marinate mutton pieces, kurma powder, lime juice and salt for 2 hours.

2 Heat oil; sauté sliced shallots, garlic and dry spices till aromatic.

3 Add diced mutton; stir-fry for 2-3 minutes. Gradually, pour in thin coconut milk and continue stirring.

4 When the mutton is almost tender, put in potatoes and dried assam. Cook till potatoes are tender.

5 Combine the thick coconut milk, tomatoes, onions, red chillies, green chillies and pounded ingredients. Season to taste.

6 Cook till gravy is boiling; simmer for 3 minutes. Remove and dish out into a casserole. Serve hot.

STIR-FRIED MIXED VEGETABLES

Serves 4

½ *kai choy* leaf (cut lengthwise)
1 carrot (sliced)
5 cauliflower florets (cut into
  small pieces)
5 broccoli florets (cut small)
200 g snowpeas/kacang kara
  (strings removed)
a little green capsicum (cut
  into wedges)
5 button mushrooms
a few dried Chinese
  mushrooms (soaked &
  drained)
2 abalone mushrooms
a few straw mushrooms
1 teaspoon chopped garlic
2 slices ginger
1 teaspoon
  cornflour   } thoroughly
1 tablespoon water   mixed
3 tablespoons oil
sufficient water

SEASONING INGREDIENTS
1 teaspoon granulated chicken
  stock
2 tablespoons oyster sauce
100 ml stock water

1 Boil water and add in
1 tablespoonful oil. Scald *kai
choy*, sliced carrots, cauliflower,
broccoli, snowpeas, capsicum
and mushrooms.

2 Remove vegetables and dip
in cold water. Drain water.

3 Heat 2 tablespoonfuls oil.
Sauté chopped garlic and sliced
ginger until lightly browned.

4 Add in the vegetables and
cook over high heat. Add in the
seasoning ingredients and stir
well. Thicken the sauce by
adding in the cornflour mixture.

5 Remove from heat. Transfer
to a casserole and serve hot.

BHUJIA LADIES' FINGERS

Serves 4

60 ml. oil
1 large onion (halved & thinly sliced)
½ teaspoon mustard seeds/ biji sawi
2 cloves garlic (thinly sliced)
1½ cm. ginger (finely shredded)
½ teaspoon turmeric powder }
2 teaspoons cummin powder } mixed with water to a paste
300 g. ladies' fingers (sliced slantwise ½ cm.)
1 teaspoon *asam jawa* }
100 ml. water } mixed & strained
1 green chilli (chopped)
2 tomatoes (seeded & diced)
1 teaspoon sugar
2 teaspoons *garam masala*
salt to taste

1 Heat oil; stir-fry sliced onions till crisp. Remove from wok.

2 Sauté mustard seeds, sliced garlic and ginger for 1 minute. Add turmeric paste; stir well.

3 When the oil floats, combine ladies' fingers. Mix for 2-3 minutes.

4 Pour in *asam jawa* juice. Cover dish and cook till ladies' fingers become tender.

5 Combine chopped green chillies, tomatoes, sugar and salt. Stir for 2 minutes; add *garam masala* and fried onions. Remove from heat.

6 Serve ladies' fingers with boiled white rice and fresh bread.

TOMATO RICE

Serves 4

50 g. ghee
2 tablespoons oil
4 cm. cinnamon stick
3 star anise
1 large onion ⎫
4 shallots ⎬ **blended**
3 cloves garlic ⎭ **to a paste**
2 *pandan* leaves (knotted)
500 g. *Basmathi* rice (washed
  & drained)
700 ml. hot water
100 ml. evaporated milk
125 ml. tomato puree
salt to taste
40 g. roasted ⎫
  cashew nuts ⎬ **for**
40 g. fried shallots ⎬ **garnishing**
40 g. raisins ⎭

1 Heat ghee and oil. Fry cinnamon stick and star anise till aromatic.

2 Mix in blended paste; stir till light brown.

3 Add *pandan* leaves and rice. Cook for 3 minutes.

4 Combine the hot water, milk, tomato puree and salt. Stir occasionally till almost dry.

5 Cover pot, then reduce heat. Leave to cook completely.

6 Serve rice with cashew nuts, fried shallots and raisins.

TIPS
To maintain the crispness of the fried shallots, add a little salt to them while they are still hot (as soon as they are taken out of the frying pan).

SPICY FRIED CHICKEN

Serves 4-6

1 kg. chicken wings
1 tablespoon thick *asam jawa*
  juice
100 g. cornflour
200 g. Chinese celery
  (chopped) } for garnishing
chilli sauce (for serving)
salt & sugar to taste
oil for frying

BLENDED INGREDIENTS

6 shallots
3 cm. ginger
4 cloves garlic
1 teaspoon white
  pepper powder
3 tablespoons curry
  powder   } a little
                    water
2 tablespoons chilli   added
  paste
1 teaspoon turmeric
  powder/kunyit

1 Combine chicken wings with thick *asam jawa* juice, cornflour, salt, sugar and the blended ingredients. Allow to marinate for 2 hours.

2 Heat oil; deep-fry the chicken wings till golden brown and crispy.

3 Remove from heat and drain on paper towel.

4 Serve hot fried chicken with chopped celery and chilli sauce.

TIPS
Spices such as white pepper, fennel powder, coriander, etc. should be dry-fried to improve the aroma and then blended dry. After that, mix it with the blended wet ingredients (shallots, ginger, lemon grass, etc.)

CLAYPOT RICE

Serves 4

1 chicken wing/chicken thigh
2 slices ginger
1 teaspoon minced garlic
220 g rice
500 ml water
2 mushrooms (soaked and
  quartered)
100 g. salted fish (washed and
  drained)
some prawns (shelled and
  de-veined)
1 teaspoon fried shallots
some dried cuttlefish (thinly
  sliced)
2 stalks mustard greens/sawi
  (cut lengthwise and scalded)
sufficient oil

SEASONING INGREDIENTS
1 tablespoon light soya sauce
1 teaspoon thick soya sauce
1 teaspoon sesame oil
1 tablespoon oyster sauce

1 Clean the chicken. Debone it and cut into pieces.

2 Heat oil; sauté ginger slices and minced garlic until golden.

3 Add in seasoning ingredients; mix thoroughly. Remove and season chicken pieces with seasoning for 15 minutes.

4 Wash the rice. Pour rice into the claypot, add water and leave to cook over low heat for 15 minutes until the water dries up.

5 Add in the remaining ingredients, except for the mustard greens. Cover pot and cook for a further 15 minutes.

6 Remove pot from the stove and add in the mustard greens. Serve immediately.

JOHOR LAKSA

Serves 4

60 ml. oil
2 tablespoons coriander powder ⎫
1 tablespoon fennel powder ⎬ mixed with water to a paste
2 tablespoons curry powder ⎪
2 tablespoons chilli paste ⎭
2 *l* coconut milk (from 1½ coconuts)
500 g. mackerel/ikan kembung (boiled, bones & head discarded, pounded)
40 g. dried shrimps (soaked in hot water & pounded)
1 tablespoon *asam jawa* ⎫ combined & strained
50 ml. water ⎭
8 sprigs *daun kesum*
salt & sugar to taste

ACCOMPANIMENTS
500 g. fresh yellow noodles/ mee (scalded)
6-8 *kasturi* limes (halved)
300 g. bean sprouts (tailed)
2 large onions ⎫ thinly sliced
1 cucumber ⎭
40 g. *daun selom* ⎫ finely chopped
40 g. *daun selasih* ⎭

SAMBAL BELACAN INGREDIENTS
6 red chillies ⎫
2 cm. dried shrimp paste/belacan (roasted) ⎬ blended to a paste
salt & sugar to taste ⎭

BLENDED INGREDIENTS
8 shallots
4 cloves garlic
3 cm. ginger
3 cm. galangal
2 stalks lemon grass

1 Sauté the blended paste in hot oil till aromatic.

2 Mix in the spice mixture, stirring occasionally.

3 When the oil floats, add in coconut milk. Cook, stirring till it boils. Then combine pounded fish, prawns, *assam* juice and *daun kesum*.

4 As soon as the gravy boils again, reduce heat and simmer till the oil rises to the top. Season to taste.

5 To serve, place noodles in small bowls. Add garnishing ingredients and serve with *sambal belacan* and *kasturi* limes.

TIPS
Yellow noodles/mee may be substituted with spaghetti. For one person, the estimated amount of spaghetti (dry) is 80 grams.

AYAM GOLEK *(Stuffed Chicken)*

Serves 4-6

1 chicken
1 piece chicken liver ⎱ diced
1 piece chicken gizzard ⎰ small
1.2 l coconut milk (from 2 coconuts)
1 piece dried assam
1 potato (peeled, boiled & diced)
7 quails' eggs (boiled & shelled)
100 ml ghee
salt & sugar to taste

BLENDED INGREDIENTS
3 large onions
6 cloves garlic
3 cm. ginger
2 cm. galangal/lengkuas
2 tablespoons fennel ⎫
2 tablespoons coriander ⎬ dry-fried
1 tablespoon white peppercorn ⎭

3 Add chicken liver and gizzard into the wok. Stir till cooked through.

4 Remove from heat; mix with the diced potatoes and quails' eggs. Season to taste with salt and sugar.

6 Sew the opening to enclose the stuffing.

7 Tie the chicken's legs together. Steam the chicken for 40-45 minutes or till cooked.

1 Heat ghee in a wok. Stir-fry the blended ingredients till the oil rises.

2 Combine half of the fried ingredients with the coconut milk.

5 Stuff the spice mixture into the chicken's cavity.

8 Bring to the boil the coconut milk and dried assam piece. Add salt and stir till the mixture boils. Place the steamed chicken into the coconut milk. Continue cooking and basting the chicken. Once the gravy thickens, remove from heat and serve.

KUIH BAHULU

Serves 8-10

**420 g. all-purpose flour
10 eggs
600 g. granulated sugar
 (ground)
1 teaspoon rose essence
oil to grease mould**

1 Dry-fry flour over low heat for 10 minutes. Leave to cool.

2 Beat eggs and sugar till very light and fluffy.

3 Add in rose essence; mix well.

4 Place half of the egg mixture in a clean bowl. Fold in half of the flour. When all is used up, mix the remaining egg mixture and flour.

5 Heat a *cermai*-shaped mould in an oven with a top and bottom heating element at 225°C.

6 Tie a few *pandan* leaves together. Cut the untied ends to

form a brush. Dip this end into some oil, then grease the mould.

7 Spoon the egg mixture into the mould till three-quarters full.

8 Bake for 8-10 minutes or till the sides are golden brown. Grill for about 2 minutes or till the top part of the *bahulu* is light brown.

9 Remove from oven and serve. When cool, *kuih bahulu* may be stored in airtight containers.

TIPS
Frying the all-purpose flour without oil will reduce its dampness. The cake will rise easily and will last long.

CENDOL

Serves 4

1 *l* coconut milk
  (from 1½ coconuts) }mixed
a pinch of salt

CENDOL INGREDIENTS

20 screwpine/pandan } blended &
  leaves   strained
500 ml. water
a dash of green colouring
1 teaspoon slaked lime water/air
  kapur
150 g. green bean flour
1 tablespoon rice flour
430 ml. water

SYRUP INGREDIENTS

300 g. palm sugar/gula melaka
  (finely chopped)
100 g. granulated sugar
250 ml. water
2 screwpine/pandan leaves
  (knotted)

1 **To prepare** *cendol***:** Combine *pandan* juice, green colouring, slaked lime water, green bean flour, rice flour and water till a smooth batter is obtained. Stir mixture over medium heat till thick and shiny.

2 Fill a large bowl with cold water. Place the *cendol* mould on the bowl.

3 Transfer the cooked mixture into the mould. Press mixture with the back of a wooden spoon. Allow the strands of *cendol* formed to drop into the water.

4 Set aside for 15 minutes before straining. Refrigerate *cendol*.

5 **To prepare syrup:** Combine all the ingredients; bring to the boil. When all the sugars have dissolved, remove and leave to cool.

6 To serve, spoon *cendol* into a glass. Add ice cubes. Pour in coconut milk, followed by the palm sugar syrup.

PRAWN SAMBAL WITH PETAI

Serves 3-4

50 ml. oil
1 tablespoon thick *asam jawa*
 juice
3 tablespoons chilli sauce
a little water
200 g. medium-sized prawns
 (shelled & tails intact)
150 g. *petai* (halved)
1 tomato (cut into 6 wedges)
1 large onion (sliced into rings)
salt & sugar to taste

BLENDED INGREDIENTS
6 shallots
4 cloves garlic
1-2 tablespoons chilli paste
1 cm. dried shrimp paste/
 belacan

1 Heat oil; stir-fry the blended ingredients till aromatic.

2 Combine *asam jawa* juice, chilli sauce and some water.

3 When the oil floats, add the prawns and *petai*. Stir for 3-4 minutes.

4 Adjust seasoning to taste. If the gravy is too thick, add a little water.

5 When the prawns are cooked, put in the tomato wedges and onion rings.

6 Stir for a further 2 minutes. Dish up and serve immediately.

SWEET AND SOUR FISH

Serves 4

600 g siakap fish
½ large onion (thinly sliced)
1-2 red chillies (sliced thinly &
lengthwise)
oil for deep-frying

MARINADE INGREDIENTS
a pinch of cornflour
1 egg white

SEASONING INGREDIENTS
2 tablespoons sour plum sauce
3 tablespoons tomato sauce
2 *kasturi* limes
250 ml water
1 tablespoon oil

1 Clean the fish. Dry with a cloth.

2 Mix the marinade ingredients and marinade the fish for 15 minutes.

3 Heat a lot of oil in a wok. Fry the fish over low heat until both sides are golden brown. Remove and drain.

4 Place fish in the middle of a serving platter. Arrange the sliced onions and red chillies on the fish.

5 Heat 1 tablespoonful oil; add in the seasoning ingredients. Mix well and leave to boil.

6 Ladle the sauce and gently pour onto the fish. Serve hot with boiled, white rice.

SOTO AYAM

Serves 6-8

1 chicken (halved)
2.5 *l* water
3 tablespoons oil
5 cm. galangal/lengkuas (coarsely pounded)
2 stalks lemon grass/serai (bruised)
2 star anise (2 petals finely pounded)
12 cloves
¾ teaspoons nutmeg powder
15 shallots ⎫ thinly sliced & fried
5 cloves garlic ⎭ separately till crisp
1 teaspoon black pepper powder
salt & sugar to taste

ACCOMPANIMENTS
300 g. bean sprouts (tailed & blanched)
300 g. compressed rice (diced)
50 g. transparent noodles/suun (deep fried)
500 g. fresh yellow noodles/mee (scalded)
6 stalks spring onion ⎫ chopped
6 stalks celery ⎭
2 cakes bean curd (fried & sliced)

MEAT PATTIES INGREDIENTS
200 g. minced meat
300 g. potatoes (boiled, peeled & mashed)
5 stalks Chinese celery (finely chopped)
4 shallots (thinly sliced, fried crisp & pounded)
¼ teaspoon black pepper powder
salt to taste
1 egg (beaten)
oil for deep-frying

CHILLI SAUCE INGREDIENTS
8-10 bird's eye chillies/cili padi ⎫ blended
2 green chillies ⎭
3 tablespoons sweet soya sauce
1 cm. dried shrimp paste/belacan
a little water
salt & sugar to taste

1 Bring to the boil chicken and water in a large pot.

2 Sauté galangal, lemon grass, star anise and cloves in hot oil for 1 minute.

3 Combine ingredients in a pot. Add nutmeg powder, then season to taste. Leave till the chicken is cooked through.

4 Remove chicken and shred the meat. Add the bones into the soup. Mix in one-third of the fried shallots and black pepper powder. Boil for 10 minutes.

5 Discard the bones and season to taste.

6 To prepare meat patties: Combine all ingredients, shape into rounds and flatten slightly. Dip into beaten egg. Deep-fry patties in hot oil till golden brown. Remove.

7 To prepare chilli sauce: Mix well and place in a small bowl.

8 Divide yellow noodles and compressed rice in individual bowls. Top with chicken, bean sprouts, transparent noodles, spring onions, celery and bean curd.

9 Ladle hot soup over noodles and sprinkle remaining fried shallots and garlic on top. Serve at once.

AYAM KURMA

Serves 4-6

1 chicken (cut into 10-12 pieces)
4 tablespoons oil
4 cm. cinnamon stick ⎫
2 cloves   ⎬ dry spices
4 star anise   ⎪
2 cardamoms ⎭
6 shallots ⎫
4 cloves garlic ⎬ blended to a paste
2 cm. ginger ⎪
½ large onion ⎭
3 tablespoons *kurma* powder (mixed with water to a paste)
3 candlenuts/buah keras (finely pounded)
1.2 l coconut milk (from 1 coconut)
1 slice dried assam
3 medium potatoes (peeled & quartered)
3 tomatoes ⎫ quartered
2 large onions ⎭
2 green chillies ⎫ halved lengthwise, do not split
2 red chillies ⎭
salt to taste

1 Heat oil and sauté the dry spices for 1 minute.

2 Add in the blended paste; stir till light brown.

3 Combine *kurma* paste and candlenuts; mix till the oil floats.

4 Put in chicken pieces and mix well. Gradually pour in the coconut milk.

5 Stir occasionally until the gravy boils. Add the assam slice, potatoes and salt to taste.

6 When the potatoes are almost tender, put in tomatoes, onions, green and red chillies.

7 Cook until the oil rises to the top. Dish up onto a serving platter and serve.

TIPS
If you wish to reduce the amount of fat in this dish, discard the chicken skin before cooking.

DAGING MASAK MERAH ALA THAI

Serves 4

500 g. tender cut beef
sufficient water (to boil beef)
a dash of red colouring
60 ml. oil
2 cloves garlic (minced)
2 teaspoons dried
  shrimp paste powder ⎫
1 tablespoon fish sauce ⎬ mixed
½ tablespoon sugar   with
4 tablespoons   100 ml.
  tomato sauce   water
3 tablespoons chilli
  sauce ⎭
6 stalks spring onion (cut into 3
  cm. lengths)
2 large onions (sliced into rings)
2 tomatoes (cut into 6 wedges)
2 red chillies (cut slantwise)
4-5 bird's eye chillies/cili padi
  (bruised)
1 teaspoon cornflour ⎫ mixed
3 tablespoons water ⎭
salt to taste

1 Boil beef in water and red colouring till tender.

2 Remove; leave to cool slightly, then slice beef thinly.

3 Heat oil and sauté minced garlic till fragrant.

4 Add in the sauce mixture. Stir well and season to taste.

5 Combine the beef slices, spring onions, onion rings, tomatoes, red chillies, *cili padi* and cornflour mixture.

6 Mix thoroughly till the gravy thickens. Dish up and serve hot.

BERGEDEL DAGING (Meat Patties)

Serves 6

300 g. potatoes (boiled, peeled
   & mashed)
100 g. shallots (thinly sliced,
   fried crisp & pounded)
200 g. minced meat
5 stalks celery ⎫
5 stalks spring onion ⎬ minced
1 tablespoon coriander
   powder
½ tablespoon fennel powder
1 teaspoon cummin powder
1 teaspoon white pepper
   powder
salt to taste
4 eggs
oil for frying

1 Mix mashed potatoes, fried shallots, minced meat, celery, spring onions, coriander powder, fennel powder, cummin powder, white pepper powder and salt.

2 Shape into balls and flatten a little.

3 Add salt to eggs and beat slightly.

4 Heat oil. Dip patties in egg and deep-fry over low heat. When patties are cooked and golden brown, remove and drain well on paper towel.

5 Serve hot with chilli sauce, if preferred.

PECAL

Serves 4-6

60 g. long beans ⎤
100 g. tapioca   ⎥ cut 2 cm. &
  shoots   ⎥ blanched
100 g. *kangkung* ⎦ separately

1 large cucumber (discard soft
  part & cut into small pieces)
100 g. bean sprouts (tailed &
  scalded)
3 cakes bean curd (fried &
  thinly sliced)

GRAVY INGREDIENTS
2 tablespoons oil
6-8 dried chillies (seeded)
5 shallots (quartered)
2 cloves garlic (halved)
3 tablespoons dried prawns
  (soaked & drained)
1 cm. dried shrimp paste cube
200 g. groundnuts (dry-fried,
  skinned & ground)
2 tablespoons *asam* ⎤
  jawa   ⎥ mixed &
400-450 ml. hot   ⎥ strained
  water   ⎦
salt & sugar to taste

1 Arrange all the vegetables and bean curd on a large serving platter.

2 **To prepare gravy:** Heat oil. Stir-fry dried chillies, shallots, garlic and dried prawns till golden brown. Remove and drain on paper towel.

3 Blend fried shallots mixture and dried shrimp paste till fine.

4 Transfer to a bowl. Put in the groundnuts and *asam jawa* juice. Add more hot water if gravy is too thick.

5 Season to taste. Serve with the assorted vegetables.

KAI LAN WITH BEEF

Serves 4

400 g. beef
3 slices young ginger
1 tablespoon chopped garlic
500 g. *kai lan* (washed and cut
  lengthwise)
100 ml stock water
1 teaspoon cornflour ⎱ mixed
1 tablespoon water ⎰ thoroughly
oil (for frying & sautéing)

MARINADE INGREDIENTS
1 tablespoon ginger juice
a pinch of cornflour

SEASONING INGREDIENTS
1 tablespoon chicken stock
  granules
2 tablespoons oyster sauce
2 teaspoons Worcestershire
  sauce

1 Wash beef and dry with a cloth. Slice thinly following the vein. Mix beef thoroughly with the marinade ingredients and leave for 15 minutes.

2 Heat sufficient oil. Add in beef and fry over high heat until half-cooked. Remove and drain.

3 Leave 2 tablespoonfuls oil in wok. Sauté the ginger and garlic till browned. Add in beef and stir-fry over high heat for a while. Put in seasoning ingredients and *kai lan*. Mix well.

4 Pour in the stock and leave to simmer. Thicken the gravy with cornflour mixture.

5 Remove and transfer to a serving plate. Serve hot.

Nasi Minyak

Serves 4

70 g. ghee
5 cm. cinnamon stick ⎫ dry
2 cloves ⎬ spices
2 cardamoms ⎭
5 shallots ⎫ blended to
3 cloves garlic ⎬ a paste
2 cm. ginger ⎭
500 g. *Basmathi* rice (washed
   & drained)
1 *pandan* leaf (knotted)
¼ teaspoon turmeric powder/
   kunyit
750 ml. water
100 ml. evaporated milk
salt to taste
40 g. roasted ⎫
   cashew nuts ⎬ for
40 g. fried shallots ⎬ garnishing
60 g. green peas ⎭

1 Sauté the dry spices in hot ghee for 2 minutes.

2 Mix in the blended paste; stir till fragrant.

3 Combine the rice, *pandan* leaf and turmeric powder. Cook, stirring for 3 minutes.

4 Pour in the water, milk and salt. Stir occasionally till boiling.

5 As soon as the rice has absorbed most of the water, cover the pot and reduce heat. Leave to cook for 10 minutes.

6 Sprinkle the garnishing ingredients on top of rice. Serve immediately.

HAILAM CHICKEN RICE

Serves 4

1 chicken (cleaned & drained)
2 cm ginger (crushed)
2 teaspoons salt
a dash of sesame oil
sufficient water (for boiling and scalding)
1 bulb garlic }**chopped**
2 shallots
440 g. fragrant rice (washed and drained)
1 screwpine leaf/daun pandan
2 tablespoons oil

CHICKEN SAUCE INGREDIENTS
1 teaspoon sugar
1 teaspoon seasoning powder
1 teaspoon sesame oil } **well-mixed**
2 tablespoons light soya sauce
200 ml. chicken stock

SERVING SAUCE INGREDIENTS
100 g. chopped ginger
50 g. chopped garlic
50 g. chopped shallots
200 g. chopped chillies } **well-mixed**
5 *kasturi* limes (juice extracted)
sugar and salt to taste
a dash of tomato sauce

1 Boil sufficient water to cover chicken. Add in crushed ginger and salt to taste. Simmer gently.

2 Lower heat and add in chicken. Leave to simmer for about 45 minutes.

3 Remove chicken and immerse in cold water for about 20-30 minutes. Remove and drain.

4 Brush chicken with sesame oil. Put aside.

5 Heat oil and sauté the chopped garlic and shallots until fragrant. Add in rice and mix thoroughly.

6 Transfer rice to a rice cooker. Pour in the water that was used to boil the chicken. Put in screwpine leaf. Leave until rice is cooked.

7 Cut chicken into sections. Pour chicken sauce carefully on top of the chicken. Serve the rice with the serving sauce.

SAMOSAS

Serves 6-8

DOUGH INGREDIENTS
250 g. all-purpose flour
2 teaspoons baking powder
½ teaspoon salt
½ teaspoon turmeric powder/
serbuk kunyit
1 teaspoon cummin powder
1 teaspoon chilli powder
2 tablespoons ghee
sufficient cold water
oil for deep-frying

FILLING INGREDIENTS
2 tablespoons oil
1 large onion } finely
2 cloves garlic } chopped
2 teaspoons } mixed
  fennel powder } with
1½ tablespoons } water to
  curry powder } a paste
100 g. green peas
1 red chilli } finely chopped
1 green chilli }
400 g. potatoes (peeled, diced
  & boiled)
juice of 1 lime
salt & sugar to taste

2 Put in green peas, chopped chillies, potatoes and lime juice. Season to taste with salt and sugar. Combine well and remove from heat. Set filling aside to cool.

6 Cut into a 6 x 25 cm. rectangle.

3 **To prepare dough:** Mix all the dry ingredients. Rub in ghee.

7 Spoon some filling on one end of the dough. Fold in a triangular shape till the end.

4 Gradually add in water. Knead gently to a soft dough.

8 Seal the ends of dough with some water. Deep-fry *samosas* in hot oil till golden and crispy.

1 **To prepare filling:** Heat oil; sauté chopped onions and garlic till fragrant. Add curry powder paste; stir for 1 minute.

5 Roll out dough thinly on a board.

SERUNDING DAGING (*Beef Floss*)

Serves 4

500 g. beef (boiled tender &
   shredded)
1 grated coconut
500 ml. thick coconut milk (from
   1 coconut)
4 tablespoons chilli powder
2 tablespoons
   coriander   ⎫
1 tablespoon fennel ⎬ dry fried
1 tablespoon cummin ⎭ & ground
2 tablespoons sugar
3 turmeric leaves/daun kunyit
   (knotted)
salt to taste

BLENDED INGREDIENTS
10 g. shallots
50 g. garlic
30 g. ginger
3 stalks lemon grass/serai
2 cm. galangal/lengkuas

1 Dry-fry grated coconut till golden brown. Then pound or blend till an oily paste (*kerisik*) is obtained.

2 Combine all the ingredients and stir over medium heat. Adjust seasoning. Be careful as the dish dries up and may become too salty.

3 When the gravy thickens, reduce heat. Keep on stirring till the mixture is dark brown and crispy.

4 Discard the turmeric leaves. Dish up and serve with *lemang* or *ketupat*.

SUP TULANG *(Ox Bone Soup)*

Serves 4-6

1 kg. ox bone (cut to desired size)
2 *l*. water
2 tablespoons oil
1 large onion (thinly sliced)
3 tablespoons light soya sauce
salt & black pepper to taste
5 stalks Chinese celery (finely chopped)
10 shallots (thinly sliced & fried crisp)

SPICE INGREDIENTS
4 cloves garlic ⎫ **bruised**
5 cm. ginger ⎭
1 star anise
6 cardamoms
6 cm. cinnamon stick
1 teaspoon fennel powder
1 teaspoon cummin powder
1 teaspoon coriander powder
1 teaspoon white pepper powder

1 Bring to the boil ox bones, water and spice ingredients. Simmer for 1½ hours or until bones are tender. Add more water if necessary.

2 Remove bones and strain the soup.

3 Heat oil; fry sliced onions till golden brown and fragrant.

4 Add the ox bones, soup, soya sauce, salt and black pepper.

5 When the soup boils, remove from heat. Garnish with chopped celery and fried shallots. Serve hot.

OPOR AYAM

Serves 4-6

1 chicken (cut into 8 pieces)
800 ml. coconut milk (from 1
  coconut)
2 stalks lemon grass/serai
  (bruised)
3 daun limau purut/lime leaves
1 teaspoon *asam jawa* } **mixed &**
50 ml. water } **strained**
salt & sugar to taste

BLENDED INGREDIENTS
6 cloves garlic
1 large onion
3 cm. galangal/lengkuas
3 cm. ginger
2 stalks lemon grass/serai

GROUND INGREDIENTS
3 tablespoons coriander } **dry-**
1 tablespoon fennel } **fried**
4 candlenuts/buah keras

1 Marinate chicken pieces with the blended and ground ingredients for 1 hour.

2 Place coconut milk, lemon grass, *daun limau purut*, salt and sugar in a large pot. Bring to the boil; stirring occasionally.

3 Put in *asam jawa* juice and chicken pieces.

4 Mix thoroughly till the chicken pieces are well-cooked. Season to taste with salt and sugar.

5 When the *opor* gravy thickens slightly, remove from heat and serve.

YAU CHA KWAI

Serves 8

YEAST DOUGH INGREDIENTS
200 g. plain flour
300 ml. warm water
1 tablespoon instant yeast

DOUGH INGREDIENTS
**1½ teaspoons alum/*pak fun*
  (pounded)**
 400 ml. water
2 teaspoons ammonia powder
**1½ teaspoons bicarbonate
  soda**
2 teaspoons salt
2 tablespoons oil
600 g. high protein flour
1 tablespoon oil (for coating)
**2-3 tablespoons plain flour (for
  sprinkling)**
oil for deep-frying

1 **To prepare yeast dough:**
Combine all the ingredients well.
Cover with a damp tea towel. Leave
for 1-2 hours.

2 Dissolve alum with half of the
water. Then mix with the yeast
dough.

3 Combine the remaining water
with ammonia powder, bicarbonate
soda and salt.

4 Then mix well the yeast dough,
ammonia mixture and oil.

5 Knead in the flour till a soft
but pliable dough is obtained. Cover
with a damp tea towel. Set aside for
30 minutes.

6 Knead the dough again for 10
minutes. Then coat dough with some
oil. Leave for 2 more hours.

7 Sprinkle flour on the work
surface. Roll dough into a 30 cm x
10 cm rectangle. Cut into 20 strips,
each measuring 1.5 cm x 10 cm.

8 Dip a bamboo skewer in water.
Then wet half the strip (lengthwise)
with the skewer. Place the other half
strip on top of the wet one. Repeat
the process till all the dough is used
up.

9 Heat oil in the wok.

10 Lift the joined strips, stretch
them a little, then lower into the hot
oil. Fry, turning often till golden
brown. Remove with a slotted spoon
and drain well.

KAMBING KEEMA *(Mutton Keema)*

Serves 4

225 g. minced mutton
3 tablespoons meat curry
 powder
salt to taste
5 tablespoons oil
2 large onions (diced small)
4 cardamoms (bruised)
5 cloves
1 star anise
2 cm. cinnamon stick
1 cm. ginger ⎫
2 cloves garlic ⎬ **pounded**
500 ml. thin coconut milk
 (from ½ coconut)
2 potatoes ⎫ **diced 2 cm.**
2 tomatoes ⎭
60 g. green peas
2 sprigs coriander leaves/daun
 ketumbar (finely chopped)
sugar to taste

1 Combine minced mutton, curry powder and salt. Set aside for 10 minutes.

2 Heat oil; sauté diced onions till fragrant.

3 Add cardamoms, cloves, star anise, cinnamon stick, ginger, garlic and mutton. Stir till mixture is quite dry.

4 Gradually pour in 125 ml coconut milk. When boiling, simmer for 5 minutes.

5 Put in diced potatoes and the remaining coconut milk. Continue stirring till the potatoes are soft; put in diced tomatoes and peas.

6 Adjust seasoning to taste and remove. Serve mutton *keema*, garnished with chopped coriander leaves.

SPICY FRIED PRAWNS

Serves 3-4

500 g. tiger prawns
60 ml. oil
1 stalk curry leaves/daun kari
1 large onion (diced small)
5 shallots ⎫
3 cloves garlic ⎬ blended
1 stalk lemon ⎪
  grass/serai ⎭
2 tablespoons ⎫
  coriander powder ⎪
1 tablespoon fennel ⎪
  powder ⎪
½ tablespoon ⎬ combined
  cummin powder ⎪
1 teaspoon chilli ⎪
  powder ⎪
½ teaspoon ⎭
  turmeric powder
1 teaspoon lime juice
salt & sugar to taste

1 Marinate prawns with blended paste, mixed spices, sugar and salt for 30 minutes.

2 Heat oil; sauté curry leaves and diced onions till golden.

3 Add the prawns and stir till half-cooked.

4 Mix in the lime juice and combine for 1 minute. Adjust seasoning to taste.

5 Stir the mixture and dish up onto a serving platter. Serve.

PACERI NANAS

Serves 3-4

700 g. half-ripe pineapple
  (sliced)
100 ml. water
3 tablespoons oil
2 cloves
4 cm. cinnamon stick
1 stalk curry leaf/daun kari
6 shallots ⎫ thinly
2 cm. ginger ⎰ sliced
2 tablespoons dried prawns
  (soaked & pounded)
3 tablespoons meat curry
  powder (mixed with water to
  a paste)
2 tablespoons *kerisik* (pounded
  crispy-fried grated coconut)
800 ml. coconut milk (from 1
  coconut)
2 tablespoons brown sugar/gula
  merah
1 piece dried assam
salt to taste

1 Boil pineapple slices in water till soft. Drain well and set aside.

2 Sauté cloves, cinnamon stick and curry leaf in hot oil for 1 minute.

3 Add in sliced shallots and ginger; fry till fragrant.

4 Combine dried prawns, curry powder, *kerisik* and salt. Stir till the oil rises.

5 Gradually, add in the coconut milk, brown sugar and dried assam.

6 When gravy boils, simmer till slightly thick.

7 Put in the sliced pineapples. Adjust seasoning and return to the boil.

8 Dish up into a casserole and serve hot.

DHAL CURRY

Serves 4

150 g. yellow dhal (cleaned & soaked for 2 hours)
½ teaspoon turmeric powder/ serbuk kunyit
sufficient water to cover dhal
1 large tomato (diced small)
1 tablespoon oil
1 stalk curry leaves/daun kari
¼ teaspoon mustard seeds/ biji sawi
a pinch of fenugreek/halba
2 large onions ⎫
1 cm. ginger ⎬ **finely chopped**
2 cloves garlic ⎭
½ tablespoon chilli powder
1 green chilli (seeded & finely chopped)
salt to taste

1 Boil dhal, turmeric powder and water till the dhal is tender. The mixture should not be too thick.

2 Combine diced tomatoes and salt; reduce the heat.

3 Heat oil; stir-fry curry leaves, mustard seeds and fenugreek for 1 minute.

4 Put in chopped green chillies and stir well.

5 Tip mixture into the dhal. Combine thoroughly and cover pan for 5 minutes. Season well with salt.

6 Dish up into a casserole. Serve dhal curry with *roti canai* or *chapati*.

FRIED CHOY TAM

Serves 4

600 g. *choy tam*
2 tablespoons sliced garlic
3 tablespoons oil
sufficient water

SEASONING INGREDIENTS
2 tablespoons chicken stock
  granules
2 tablespoons oyster sauce
a pinch of salt

1 Discard old *choy tam* leaves. Halve the leaves and wash in water.

2 Boil water and add in 1 tablespoonful oil. Scald *choy tam* for only a few minutes. Remove and dip into cold water. Drain well.

3 Heat the remaining oil and sauté the sliced garlic until golden.

4 Add in *choy tam* and mix well. Put in the seasoning ingredients and fry briskly until well-mixed.

5 Remove and transfer to a serving plate. Serve immediately.

FISH CURRY

Serves 4-6

**600 g. mackerel/ikan kembung
(sliced)**
4 tablespoons oil
½ teaspoon fenugreek/halba
**½ teaspoon mustard seeds/biji
sawi**
1 stalk curry leaves/daun kari
4 shallots } **finely**
2 cloves garlic } **sliced**
**2 tablespoons fish
curry powder** } **blended
with**
**½ teaspoon
turmeric powder** } **water to
a paste**
**1 teaspoon
chilli powder** }
1 teaspoon *asam jawa* } **mixed &**
100 ml. water } **strained**
**600 ml. thin coconut
milk** } **from 1
coconut**
**200 ml. thick coconut
milk** }
300 g. ladies' fingers (trimmed)
**3 medium-sized tomatoes
(quartered)**
salt & sugar to taste

1 Heat oil; stir-fry fenugreek, mustard seeds, curry leaves, shallots and garlic till fragrant.

2 Add in curry powder mixture; stir for 2-3 minutes.

3 Gradually pour in half of the thin coconut milk, mixing occasionally till the oil separates.

4 Combine *asam jawa* juice, remaining thin coconut milk, ladies' fingers and fish slices.

5 Stir till mixture is boiling. Add in thick coconut milk, tomatoes, sugar and salt.

6 As soon as gravy boils again, reduce heat and simmer till the fish slices are cooked.

7 Dish out into a casserole. Serve hot with boiled white rice or fresh bread.

MEE SIAM

Serves 4

400 g. mee hoon/rice noodles
  (soaked till softened &
  drained)
60 ml. oil
3 tablespoons chilli sauce
2 tablespoons oyster sauce
2 tablespoons soya sauce
200 g. mustard greens/
  sawi   } sliced
10 stalks chives/   3 cm.
  daun kucai
300 g. bean sprouts (tailed)
2 cakes bean curd (fried & thinly
  sliced)
2 eggs (beaten)
salt & sugar to taste

BLENDED INGREDIENTS
5 cloves garlic
5 shallots
3 tablespoons dried shrimps
  (soaked)
6 dried chillies (cut & soaked)

TAUCHU SAUCE INGREDIENTS
2 tablespoons oil
4 shallots
2 cloves garlic   }
3 tablespoons   blended
  fermented soya   with water
  bean/taucu   to a paste
1 cm. dried shrimp   }
  paste/belacan
1 tablespoon chilli paste
salt & sugar to taste

GARNISHING INGREDIENTS
3 red chillies (cut slantwise)
3 eggs
salt to taste
1 teaspoon oil

1 Sauté the blended ingredients in hot oil till fragrant.

2 Mix in chilli sauce, oyster sauce, soya sauce, salt and sugar. Stir for 2 minutes.

3 Add the mustard greens and chives; combine for a further 2 minutes.

4 Stir in *mee hoon*, bean sprouts, bean curd and eggs. Stir until well-cooked. Dish up and serve hot with the sauce and garnishing ingredients.

5 **To prepare sauce:** Sauté the blended paste and chilli paste till fragrant. Add salt and sugar.

6 **To prepare omelette for garnishing:** Beat eggs with salt. Heat oil in a pan; fry the eggs (in two batches) as thin as possible. Remove from heat, roll eggs and slice thinly.

7 Serve *mee hoon* with red chillies, eggs and *taucu* sauce.

INDIAN FRIED MEE

Serves 4

500 g. fresh yellow noodles/mee
60 ml. oil
1 large onion (thinly sliced)
200 g. tender-cut
  mutton
  (thinly sliced)
1 tablespoon
  sweet soya sauce   } marinated
1 teaspoon dark   for 1 hour
  soya sauce
¼ teaspoon black
  pepper powder
2 tablespoons dark
  soya sauce   } seasoning
1-2 teaspoons chilli
  powder
a little water
6 tablespoons tomato sauce
8 stalks mustard greens/sawi
  (cut into 3 cm. lengths)
300 g. bean sprouts (tailed)
2 eggs (beaten)
2 green chillies (sliced)
2 tomatoes (cut into wedges)
2 potatoes (boiled & sliced
  ½ cm. thick)
3 prawn fritters (thinly sliced) }
  refer to Rojak recipe
10 shallots (finely sliced & fried
  crisp)
5 stalks spring onion (chopped)
salt to taste

1 Heat oil and sauté sliced onions till fragrant.

2 Add in the mutton slices and seasoning; stir for 3-4 minutes.

3 Pour some water over mutton and cover pan. Cook till the mutton is tender.

4 Mix in tomato sauce and mustard greens; combine for 2 minutes.

5 Put in yellow noodles, bean sprouts and beaten eggs. Stir well.

6 Add in sliced green chillies, tomatoes, potatoes and prawn fritters. Adjust seasoning to taste.

7 Remove from heat. Dish out onto a serving plate. Serve noodles, garnished with fried shallots and chopped spring onions.

KUIH KETAYAP

Serves 4-6

FILLING INGREDIENTS
40 g. palm sugar/gula melaka
    (crushed)
2 tablespoons granulated sugar
50 ml. water
½ grated coconut (reserve
    white part)

BATTER INGREDIENTS
10 screwpine/
    pandan leaves } blended &
100 ml. water   strained
250 g. all-purpose flour
½ teaspoon salt
2 eggs
450-500 ml. water
a dash of green colouring
3-4 tablespoons oil

1 To prepare filling: Bring to the boil palm sugar, sugar and water till all the sugars have dissolved.

2 Put in grated coconut and stir well. When the mixture is quite dry, remove and leave to cool.

3 Combine *pandan* juice, flour, salt, eggs and water till smooth. Strain if necessary. Then add a little green colouring.

4 Heat oil in a flat-bottomed pan. Pour in a little batter. Tilt pan round to form a thin pancake.

5 Cook over medium heat till light brown on both sides. Remove and put some coconut filling at one end of pancake.

6 Fold over opposite ends to enclose filling. Roll up neatly.

7 Arrange on a serving plate. Serve.

LEPAT PISANG

Serves 6-8

- **10 ripe pisang awak/any variety (mashed)**
- **100 ml. thick coconut milk (from ½ coconut)**
- **70 g. granulated sugar**
- **130 g. all-purpose flour**
- **60 g. grated coconut (reserve white part)**
- **½ teaspoon salt**
- **a few scalded banana leaves (12 x 22.5 cm.)**

1 Combine mashed bananas, sugar, flour, grated coconut and salt.

2 Gradually add coconut milk; stir until a smooth batter (not too thick or too thin).

3 Place about 2 tablespoonfuls mixture onto a banana leaf.

4 Fold both sides of leaf to enclose mixture. Tuck in both ends to form a neat, somewhat long rectangle.

5 Steam for 15-20 minutes or till mixture is cooked through. Transfer to a serving plate.

6 Allow *lepat pisang* to cool before serving.

IKAN PATIN MASAK TEMPOYAK

Serves 4

600 g. *ikan patin* (sliced 2 cm.)
1 teaspoon *asam jawa*
sufficient water
1 turmeric leaf/daun kunyit
4 polygonum leaves/daun kesum
salt & sugar to taste

BLENDED INGREDIENTS
8-10 bird's eye chillies/cili padi
2 red chillies
1 stalk lemon grass/serai
1.5 cm. turmeric/kunyit
1 cm. ginger
2 tablespoons fermented durian flesh/tempoyak

1 Rub fish with *asam jawa*. Set aside for 30 minutes. Clean fish and discard a*sam*.

2 Combine blended paste, water, turmeric leaf, polygonum leaves and fish slices.

3 Bring to the boil, stirring occasionally. Season to taste.

4 Simmer till the fish is cooked. Remove from heat and serve.

TIPS
If *ikan patin* is unavailable, *ikan keli* or other freshwater fish may be used. Marinate in *asam jawa* to get rid of the slime and fishy smell. To make *tempoyak*, ferment 300 grams of durian flesh with 2 tbsp salt in a lidded container and store in a dark place for 3 days. Hand-mix once each day. Then keep in a refrigerator.

LOH HON KOR

Serves 4

1 *loh hon kor*
1 kg. *labu air*
400 g. dried *longans* (washed)
800 g. brown sugar/gula
   merah
10 red dates
2 *l* water

1 Wash *loh hon kor* and crush it. Peel the skin of the *labu air* and cut into long, fine strips.

2 Bring water to the boil. Put in the *loh hon kor*, *labu air* and red dates. Cook for 30-60 minutes.

3 Add in the dried *longans* and brown sugar. Stir and leave to simmer gently for 5-10 minutes.

4 Remove from heat and allow to cool before serving in bowls.

OTAK-OTAK

Serves 4

300 g Spanish mackerel/
  tenggiri
sugar & salt to taste
60 ml water
80 g grated coconut (white
  part)
180 ml thick coconut milk
  (from 1 coconut)
several coconut leaves (cut
  into 20 cm lengths)
a few cocktail sticks/stapler

GROUND INGREDIENTS
8-10 dried chillies
5 candlenuts/buah keras
1 cm turmeric/kunyit
3 cloves garlic
10 shallots
2 cm galangal/lengkuas
1 cm dried shrimp paste/
  belacan

2 Add in the grated coconut;
mix well and season with sugar
and salt to taste.

3 Pour thick coconut milk into
the mixture.

1 Discard the skin and bones
of fish. Pound or process fish
meat with salt and water. Mix
with the ground ingredients.

4 Spoon a portion of the
mixture onto a coconut leaf
(open it up slightly).

5 Place another coconut leaf
on top to enclose the filling.

6 Secure one end of the leaf
with a cocktail stick or a stapler.
Secure the other end of the leaf
to form a neat parcel.

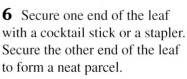

7 Continue filling the coconut
leaves till all the mixture is used
up. Grill or cook the fish parcels
over charcoal fire till cooked
through.

KUIH TALAM

Serves 6-8

BOTTOM LAYER INGREDIENTS
150 g. granulated sugar
400 ml. water
8 *pandan* leaves ⎤ blended
200 ml. water ⎦ & strained
120 g. rice flour
20 g. plain flour
1½ teaspoons slaked lime
   water/air kapur
a dash of green colouring
   (optional)

TOP LAYER INGREDIENTS
70 g. rice flour
2 tablespoons cornflour
½ teaspoon salt
350 ml. thick coconut milk (from
1 coconut)

1 To prepare bottom layer: Bring to the boil sugar. When the sugar is dissolved, remove from heat and allow to cool.

2 Combine the syrup with *pandan* juice, rice flour, plain flour, slaked lime water and green colouring until a smooth batter is formed.

3 Grease a 20 cm. baking tin with oil. Pour in batter; steam for 10-15 minutes or till batter is cooked.

4 To prepare top layer: Mix thoroughly rice flour, cornflour, salt and coconut milk till smooth.

5 Slowly pour the batter onto the bottom layer. Return to steamer and cook till it is completely set. Leave to cool before slicing *kuih talam*. Serve.

TAU FOO FA

Serves 6-8

300 g. soya beans (washed)
3 *l* water
125 ml. hot water
1 teaspoon gypsum powder
3 tablespoons cornflour

SYRUP INGREDIENTS
300 g. granulated sugar
400 ml. water
2 screwpine/pandan leaves

1 Soak soya beans overnight. Strain and discard soya bean skins.

2 Blend soya beans with 1 litre of water. Place in a muslin cloth; squeeze soya bean water into a pot.

3 Blend soya beans again with the remaining water. Strain again with muslin cloth.

4 Dissolve hot water and gypsum powder. Cool and add to the cornflour. Strain water into a large pot.

5 Bring to the boil soya bean water; stirring often. Slowly pour into the cornflour mixture, letting the water run down along the inside of the pot. Do not stir.

6 Wrap the lid of the pot with a thick towel. Cover the pot. Leave for about 1 hour or till the *tau foo fa* sets. Remove the bubbles that remain on top.

7 **To prepare syrup:** Combine sugar, water and *pandan* leaves. Bring to the boil; stirring occasionally.

8 Strain with a sieve. Serve syrup with *tau foo fa*.

TIPS
Gypsum is also known as *gesso* or *shi-gao-fen*. It can be bought at Chinese medicine shops.

PULUT KUNING (Yellow Glutinous Rice)

Serves 4-6

560 g. glutinous rice/pulut
(washed & drained)
sufficient water (to soak rice)
1 slice dried assam
2 teaspoons turmeric powder/
serbuk kunyit
2 *pandan* leaves (knotted)
250 ml. thick coconut milk
(from 1 coconut)
1½ teaspoons salt

1 **To prepare rice:** Soak glutinous rice in water, dried assam slice and turmeric powder for 4 hours or overnight.

2 Remove assam slice. Scatter the *pandan* leaves on top, then steam for 30 minutes or till rice is almost cooked.

3 Tip rice into a large bowl.

4 Add salt to coconut milk. Then combine with rice, stirring well.

5 Steam again for about 15 minutes or till cooked through.

6 Remove from steamer and serve hot.

TIPS
If the raw glutinous rice is previously soaked in a mixture of water and assam, it will turn out shiny when cooked. If desired, tumeric powder may be replaced by yellow colouring.

KERABU PUCUK PAKU

Serves 4

300 g. *pucuk paku*
sufficient water
6 shallots (finely sliced)
**6 tablespoons grated coconut
(dry-fried till crisp & pounded
to make *kerisik*)**
2-3 tablespoons lime juice
**3 tablespoons thick coconut
milk**
salt & sugar to taste
**sliced red chillies (for
garnishing)**

BLENDED INGREDIENTS
**50 g. dried prawns (soaked till
soft)**
**1 cm. dried shrimp paste/
belacan (roasted)**
4-6 bird's eye chillies/cili padi
1 slice ginger

1 Cut the tender stalks of *pucuk paku* into 2 cm. pieces. Discard hard stalks.

2 Blanch the *pucuk paku* in boiling water for 1-2 minutes. Remove then drain. Put into a large bowl.

3 Mix well the blended paste, shallots, *kerisik*, lime juice and coconut milk with the *pucuk paku*. Adjust seasoning.

4 Transfer to a plate and sprinkle red chillies before serving.

NYONYA FRIED RICE

Serves 4

1 bowl rice
1 teaspoon dried shrimps
   (soaked and drained)
4 eggs
200 g. prawns (shelled and
   deveined)
200 g. chicken breast (diced)
100 g. green peas
100 g. carrots (diced small)
1 teaspoon chopped shallots
3 tablespoons oil

SEASONING INGREDIENTS
1 teaspoon turmeric powder/
   serbuk kunyit
1 teaspoon curry powder
1 teaspoon chilli powder
1 teaspoon fish gravy
1 teaspoon light soya sauce

1 Mix the seasoning ingredients with rice. Put aside.

2 Heat oil in a wok; fry the dried shrimps over low heat until golden. Remove and keep aside.

3 Crack the eggs into the centre of the wok; fry eggs until cooked. Add in the prawns, diced chicken, green peas and chopped shallots. Mix well.

4 Add in the rice and cook for 15 minutes, mixing thoroughly.

5 When well-mixed, remove from wok. Serve immediately.

SWEET AND SOUR FISH SOUP

Serves 4

**700 g. Spanish mackerel/
tenggiri (cleaned and gutted)**
**1 tablespoon chicken stock
granules**
3 tablespoons cornflour
½ teaspoon salt
250-500 ml water

SOUP INGREDIENTS
750 ml. stock water
**1 tablespoon Chinese barbecue
sauce/sos sacha**
**1 teaspoon Worcestershire
sauce**
1 teaspoon sugar
3 tablespoons tomato sauce
2 *kasturi* limes (juice extracted)
1 teaspoon seasoning powder
a pinch of salt

1 tomato (sliced)
sufficient shredded cabbage

1 Fillet the fish. Using a spoon, separate fish meat from the skin; chop until fish is finely pounded. Keep pressing and chopping with the point of a knife.

2 Add chicken stock granules, cornflour and salt to the fish. Knead until well-mixed.

3 Beat the fish mixture against the chopping board while sprinkling it with water continuously. Repeat this process until the mixture becomes soft and pliable. Leave aside.

4 **To prepare soup:** Bring stock water to the boil; put in the fish balls using a wet teaspoon. When the balls float to the surface, remove and dip in cold water. Remove and drain.

5 Add in the remaining soup ingredients and simmer gently. Add in the fish balls, sliced tomatoes and shredded cabbage. Return soup to the boil.

6 When cooked, remove from heat. Serve hot in a soup bowl.

TANDOORI CHICKEN

Serves 6

6 chicken thighs (skin removed &
  pierced with fork)
1 large onion } blended or
3 cloves garlic } pounded
juice of 2 limes
1 teaspoon salt
1 teaspoon turmeric powder/
  serbuk kunyit
2 teaspoons chilli powder
150 g. plain yoghurt
½ teaspoon red colouring
sugar to taste
sufficient ghee

BLENDED INGREDIENTS
3-4 dried chillies (seeded &
  soaked)
1½ teaspoons mustard seeds/biji
  sawi
1 teaspoon fenugreek/halba
3 teaspoons coriander } dry-fried
1½ teaspoons cummin }

1 Marinate chicken thighs with blended onion paste, lime juice and salt for 30 minutes.

2 Combine turmeric powder, chilli powder, yoghurt, red colouring, sugar and blended ingredients.

3 Marinate chicken with the chilli mixture overnight. Place in a covered container and refrigerate.

4 Sprinkle chicken thighs with some ghee; grill or roast till chicken is cooked through.

5 Remove from grill. Transfer to a serving platter. Serve hot.

FISH HEAD CURRY

Serves 4

1 *kurau* fish head (700 g.)
200 ml. thick coconut milk ⎱ from 1½
1 *l* thin coconut milk ⎰ coconuts
5 tablespoons oil
1 teaspoon mustard seeds/biji sawi
10 shallots ⎱ pounded/
2 cloves garlic ⎰ blended
3 cm. ginger (finely shredded)
½ teaspoon fenugreek/halba
2 stalks curry leaves/daun kari
3 cm. cinnamon stick
3 round brinjals ⎱
3 tomatoes ⎰ quartered
2 green chillies
2 tablespoons ⎱ mixed &
asam jawa ⎰ strained
130 ml. water
salt to taste

SPICE INGREDIENTS
2-3 tablespoons chilli powder
2 tablespoons coriander powder
2 tablespoons cummin powder ⎱ mixed with
2 teaspoons fennel powder ⎰ water to a paste
2 teaspoons turmeric powder
½ teaspoon white pepper powder

1 Rub fish head with salt; set aside for 30 minutes. Rinse and remove salt.

2 Heat oil; fry mustard seeds till they start to 'pop'.

3 Add pounded shallots, garlic and ginger. Stir till aromatic; put in fenugreek, curry leaves, cinnamon stick and spice paste. Combine till the oil separates.

4 Gradually pour in 250 ml thin coconut milk. When boiling, add brinjals and another 250 ml thin coconut milk. Stir for 5 minutes.

5 Put in the fish head and remaining thin coconut milk. Mix well and cook till fish is almost done.

6 Combine tomatoes, green chillies, *asam jawa* juice and thick coconut milk.

7 Stir thoroughly till liquid is boiling and oil floats to the top. Adjust seasoning to taste. Dish up onto a serving dish and serve hot.

SPICY FRIED SQUIDS

Serves 4

600 g. squids (cleaned & sliced if
   large)
$\frac{1}{4}$ teaspoon white pepper powder
salt & sugar to taste
60 ml. oil

2 tablespoons chilli
   paste
2 tablespoons
   tomato puree   mixed
1 tablespoon   with
   chilli sauce   water to
2 tablespoons   a paste
   coriander powder
1 tablespoon
   fennel powder
a little water
2 tomatoes (quartered)
1 large onion (sliced into rings)
coriander leaves (finely chopped,
   for garnishing)
water

BLENDED INGREDIENTS
6 shallots
3 candlenuts/buah keras
1 cm. ginger
1 cm. galangal/lengkuas

1 Marinate squids with white
pepper, salt and sugar.

2 Heat a quarter of the oil; fry
squids till half-cooked. Remove
from wok.

3 Heat the remaining oil; sauté
blended ingredients and spice
paste till aromatic. Combine
well and add water.

4 Continue stirring till the oil
rises. Season with salt and
sugar.

5 Put in fried squids and
tomatoes. Stir completely and
dish up onto a serving platter.

6 Garnish fried squids with
chopped coriander leaves and
serve.

MEE JAWA

Serves 4

GRAVY INGREDIENTS
3 tablespoons oil
8 shallots ⎫
8 cloves garlic ⎪
2 cm. ginger ⎪
2 cm. galangal/ ⎬ **blended**
  lengkuas ⎪ **with some**
1 stalk lemon ⎪ **water to a**
  grass/serai ⎪ **paste**
1 tablespoon ⎪
  chilli paste ⎭
1.5-2 *l* water
400 g. sweet potatoes (peeled,
  boiled till soft & mashed)
300 g. prawns (shelled, boiled &
  pounded)
2 tablespoons cornflour
  (blended with some water)
½ teaspoon black pepper
  powder
sugar & salt to taste

ACCOMPANIMENTS
500 g. yellow ⎫
  noodles/mee ⎪ **scalded**
250 g. bean ⎬ **separately**
  sprouts (tailed) ⎭
4 stalks spring onion ⎫ **sliced**
4 stalks celery ⎭
2 cakes bean curd (fried &
  sliced)
4 eggs (hardboiled & halved)
4 limes (halved)
3 green/red chillies (thinly
  sliced)

1 Heat oil and stir-fry the blended paste till fragrant.

2 Add in water; stir occasionally till it is boiling.

3 Mix in sweet potatoes, prawns and cornflour mixture.

4 Bring to the boil, then simmer till gravy is thick. Season to taste with black pepper, sugar and salt.

5 Divide noodles into individual bowls. Garnish with accompaniments; then pour hot gravy on top of noodles. Serve.

NASI BERIANI HUJAN PANAS *(Colourful Rice)*

Serves 6

1 kg. *Basmathi* rice (washed & drained)
100 g. ghee
4 cm. cinnamon stick ⎫ dry
4 cardamoms   ⎬ spices
3 cloves   ⎭
3 *pandan* leaves (knotted)
1 large onion ⎫
4 shallots   ⎬ blended
3 cloves garlic ⎬ to a paste
2 cm. ginger   ⎭
40 g. *beriani* spice powder
1.4 *l* water
200 ml. evaporated milk
2 cubes beef stock (optional)
salt to taste
10 sprigs mint leaves/daun pudina
3-4 tablespoons rose water
a dash of red, orange & yellow colouring
60 g. raisins   ⎫ for
80 g. roasted   ⎬ garnishing
   almonds   ⎭

1 Heat ghee. Sauté the dry spices, *pandan* leaves and blended paste till fragrant.

2 Mix in the *beriani* spices; stir for 2-3 minutes.

3 Combine the rice and mix for 3 minutes.

4 Pour in the water and milk. Add beef stock and salt. Stir till almost dry, then scatter the mint leaves on top.

5 Lower the heat and cover the pot. Leave to cook for 10-15 minutes.

6 Sprinkle the rose water and colouring. Then cover pot completely.

7 Remove from heat. Serve hot with raisins and roasted almonds.

FRENCH BEANS WITH LIVER

Serves 4

3 tablespoons oil
4 shallots ⎫ **pounded**
2 cloves garlic ⎭
1 piece chicken liver ⎫ **finely**
1 piece chicken gizzard ⎭ **sliced**
300 g. french beans (sliced
   slantwise into 3 cm. lengths)
sufficient water
3 tablespoons oyster sauce
1 tablespoon sweet soya
   sauce
salt to taste

1 Heat oil; stir-fry the shallots and garlic till fragrant.

2 Add in chicken liver and gizzard; stir for 2-3 minutes.

3 Mix in french beans, water, oyster sauce and soya sauce. Stir and add salt to taste.

4 Stir well till the beans are quite tender.

5 Dish out onto a serving platter and serve hot.

ASPARAGUS WITH PRAWNS

Serves 4

500 g. asparagus spears
400 g. prawns (shelled and
deveined)
1 tablespoon garlic (chopped)
3 slices ginger
several button mushrooms
(finely sliced)
oil for frying

MARINADE INGREDIENTS
1 teaspoon slaked lime water/
air kapur
2 tablespoons sugar
3 tablespoons tapioca flour

SEASONING INGREDIENTS
1 tablespoon chicken stock
granules
1 tablespoon oyster sauce
2 tablespoons stock water

1 Peel outer skin of asparagus and cut into desired lengths. Keep aside.

2 Marinade prawns with the marinade ingredients for 15 minutes. Wash the prawns under running tap water for about 5 minutes. Drain.

3 Heat the oil; fry the asparagus and prawns for a short while. Remove and dip into cold water. Drain well.

4 Remove oil, leaving 2 tablespoonfuls in the wok. Sauté the chopped garlic and sliced ginger until fragrant.

5 Add in sliced button mushrooms, asparagus and prawns. Stir-fry. Put in the seasoning ingredients and stir until well-mixed.

6 Remove from heat. Dish out onto a serving plate and serve hot.

CHAPATI

Serves 4

330 g. chapati flour
¼ teaspoon salt
1½ tablespoons ghee/butter
160-170 ml. water
additional chapati flour
a little ghee

1 Mix *chapati* flour with salt. Rub in ghee.

2 Add in a little water at a time, combining till mixture holds together. Knead for 10-15 minutes or till dough is pliable.

3 Put dough into a bowl; cover with a damp towel. Set dough aside for 2 hours or overnight.

4 Shape dough into balls with a 4 cm. diameter. Flour board with *chapati* flour; roll dough into 15 cm. circles.

5 Grease a flat pan with ghee. Place *chapati* circles onto hot pan; cook for a minute. Turn over to cook other side.

6 Using a clean tea towel, press edges of chapati to 'seal' it to ensure *chapati* puffs up in the middle.

7 When cooked, remove from pan. Rub in some ghee to ensure *chapati* remains soft. Serve hot.

KUIH KOCI

Serves 6-8

500 g glutinous rice flour/
   tepung pulut
¼ teaspoon salt
450 ml. coconut milk (from 1
   coconut)
sufficient oil for dipping dough
20-25 banana leaves
   (18 x 20 cm; scalded till
   softened)

FILLING INGREDIENTS
4 tablespoons sugar
5 tablespoons brown sugar
100 ml. water
1 *pandan* leaf (knotted)
280 g. grated coconut (white
   part)

1   To prepare filling: Boil
sugar, brown sugar, water and
pandan leaf till all the sugars
have dissolved. Place grated
coconut in a wok; strain the
sugar syrup onto it. Stir over
low heat till quite dry and
remove from heat. Set aside to
cool.

2   Mix the glutinous rice flour,
salt and coconut milk to get a
soft dough.

3   Divide dough into
20-25 balls. Flatten each ball
and put in 2 teaspoonfuls filling.

4   Shape a banana leaf into a
cone.

5   Dip each filled dough ball in
some oil.

6   Place the dough ball into the
cone and press lightly.

7   Fold in the banana leaf
securely. Repeat the process till
all the dough is used up. Steam
for about 15-20 minutes or till
well-cooked.

FRIED CUTTLEFISH WITH MIXED VEGETABLES

Serves 4

600 g. cuttlefish (sliced crosswise and scalded)
2 stalks celery (strings removed and sliced at a slant)
1 red chilli (quartered)
5 slices carrot
5 button mushrooms
several straw mushrooms
5 cauliflower florets (cut small)
5 broccoli florets (cut small)
1 teaspoon chopped garlic
3 slices ginger
2 tablespoons oil

SEASONING INGREDIENTS
1 tablespoon chicken stock granules
1 tablespoon oyster sauce
a pinch of salt
125 ml. oil

1 Bring water to the boil. Scald celery, red chillies, carrots, button mushrooms, straw mushrooms, cauliflower and broccoli for a while. Remove and dip into cold water. Drain.

2 Heat oil in a wok. Sauté the chopped garlic and sliced ginger until golden in colour, then add in the scalded cuttlefish and vegetables. Stir-fry briskly.

3 Add in the seasoning ingredients. Stir until well-mixed.

4 Dish out onto a serving platter and serve hot.

NASI LEMAK WITH ANCHOVY SAMBAL

Serves 4

300 g. rice (washed & drained)
675 ml. coconut milk (from ½ coconut)
3 *pandan* leaves (knotted)
1 stalk lemon grass/serai (bruised)
salt to taste

SAMBAL INGREDIENTS
200 ml. oil
80 g. dried anchovies/ikan bilis kering (washed & drained)
1 large onion ⎫
5 shallots ⎪
3 cloves garlic ⎬ blended to
1 cm. dried shrimp paste/belacan ⎪ a paste
2 tablespoons chilli paste ⎭
1 tablespoon brown sugar/gula merah
1 teaspoon *asam jawa* ⎫ combined &
150 ml. water ⎭ strained
100 ml. chilli sauce
1 large onion (sliced into rings)
salt to taste

ACCOMPANIMENTS
100 g. groundnuts (fried in ½ teaspoonful oil)
50 g. anchovies/ikan bilis (deep-fried till crisp)
1 medium cucumber (thinly sliced)
4 eggs (hardboiled, shelled & halved)

1 Bring rice, coconut milk, pandan leaves, lemon grass and salt to the boil.

2 Stir occasionally till boiling. Cover pot and lower heat when all the water has been absorbed. Allow rice to cook completely.

3 **To prepare** *sambal*: Heat oil; stir-fry anchovies till crispy. Remove with a slotted spoon.

4 Remove half of the oil and heat the remainder. Sauté the blended paste till aromatic.

5 Mix in brown sugar, *asam jawa* juice and chilli sauce. Stir till the oil separates.

6 Lastly, add the onion rings. Season to taste with salt. When the gravy thickens, mix in the fried anchovies.

7 Serve the hot *nasi lemak* with *sambal*, groundnuts, fried anchovies, sliced cucumber and hard-boiled eggs.

YANG ZHOU FRIED RICE

Serves 4

500 g. rice
150 g. chicken breast (diced)
150 g. medium-sized prawns
  (shelled and de-veined)
3 eggs
200 g. green peas
1 small carrot (diced)
2 cloves garlic ⎫
60 g. spring onions ⎬ **minced**
200 ml. oil

SEASONING INGREDIENTS
pepper and salt to taste
a dash of light soya sauce
1 tablespoon chicken stock
  granules

1 Heat oil in wok over medium heat. Put in diced chicken and prawns. Fry until golden brown.

2 Add in eggs and mix well.

3 Put in green peas, diced carrots and minced garlic. Stir-fry for 1 minute.

4 Reduce heat. Add in rice and combine well. Sprinkle with the seasoning ingredients. Mix and turn over rice for 5-10 minutes until well-mixed.

5 Add in chopped spring onions and mix well.

6 When rice is well-mixed, transfer to a serving dish.

SERUNDING AYAM (*Chicken Floss*)

Serves 8-10

½ **grated coconut**
1 chicken (halved)
sufficient water (to cover
  chicken)
200 ml. oil
500 ml. thick coconut milk (from
  1 coconut)
2 turmeric leaves/daun kunyit
  (finely cut)
1 tablespoon thick *asam jawa*
  juice
salt & sugar to taste

BLENDED INGREDIENTS
3 tablespoons coriander (dry-
  fried)
20 shallots
2 cm. ginger
2 cm. galangal/lengkuas
8 stalks lemon grass/serai
10-12 dried chillies (soaked till
  soft)

1 Dry-fry the coconut till golden brown. Be careful not to burn it. Remove from wok, then pound or blend to make *kerisik*.

2 Boil chicken in some water till soft. Remove and shred the meat.

3 Heat oil; stir-fry the blended paste till fragrant and the oil rises.

4 Add in coconut milk, turmeric leaves, *asam jawa* juice and chicken meat. Season to taste. Do not put too much salt.

5 Stir occasionally till the mixture boils.

6 Combine the *kerisik*, then keep on stirring till mixture is very dry. Dish up or store in air-tight containers.

TIPS
Dried chillies should be snipped into 1 cm strips, the seed discarded, and soaked in hot water for 20 minutes before blending with other ingredients.

DAGING BAKAR CECAH AIR ASAM

Serves 4-6

500 g. tender cut beef (halved)
oil (to grease beef)
4 red chillies
8-10 bird's eye chillies/cili padi
2 cm. dried shrimp paste/
  belacan (roasted)
1 tablespoon *asam* ⎫
  jawa ⎬ **mixed &**
100 ml. water ⎭ **strained**
3 tablespoons sweet soya
  sauce
juice of 1-2 limes
5-6 shallots (thinly sliced)
2 tablespoons sugar
salt to taste

1 Rub oil on beef; grill or roast (preferably barbecue-style) till tender.

2 Set aside beef for 5 minutes after grilling before slicing thinly. Arrange on a serving platter.

3 Blend red chillies, *cili padi* and shrimp paste till fine.

4 Transfer to a small bowl. Combine the *asam jawa* juice, soya sauce, lime juice, shallots and sugar. Adjust seasoning to taste.

5 Serve sliced beef with the *asam* dip.

KERABU TAUGE

Serves 4

300 g. bean sprouts (tailed)
100 g. grated coconut
1 large onion (finely sliced)
4 shallots
2 red chillies
1 cm. dried shrimp paste/
   belacan (toasted)
2 tablespoons dried prawns
   (soaked)
1-2 tablespoons lime juice
1 teaspoon sugar
salt to taste

1 Blanch bean sprouts in boiling water; drain well and set aside.

2 Dry-fry grated coconut till golden brown. Remove from heat.

3 Pound or process shallots, red chillies, dried shrimp paste and dried prawns till fine.

4 Add the dry-fried grated coconut; pound until well-combined.

5 Mix well the pounded mixture, sliced onions, lime juice, salt and sugar.

6 Serve *kerabu* as an accompaniment to boiled white rice and other side dishes.

KETAM MASAK LEMAK CILI PADI

Serves 4

1 kg. crabs (halved if large)
1 *l* coconut milk (from 1
 coconut)
1 stalk lemon grass/serai
 (bruised)
1 slice dried assam
salt & sugar to taste

BLENDED INGREDIENTS
12-15 bird's eye chillies/
 cili padi
2 red chillies
6 shallots
1 cm. turmeric/kunyit

1 Combine coconut milk, lemon grass and blended ingredients. Stir till gravy is boiling.

2 Add in crabs and dried assam. Adjust seasoning to taste.

3 Stir occasionally till it boils again.

4 When the crabs are cooked and the gravy is quite thick, remove from heat.

5 Dish out onto a plate and serve hot with boiled white rice.

NASI KERABU

Serves 4

300 g. rice (washed & drained)
675 ml. water
10-15 *bunga talang* (pounded &
 squeezed to extract juice)
a dash of blue colouring
budu
fried fish crackers
boiled salted eggs
sliced lime

COCONUT SAMBAL INGREDIENTS
½ grated coconut
1 large mackerel/ikan kembung
 (grilled or baked)
5 shallots ⎱
½ teaspoon black ⎰ pounded or
 pepper powder   blended
salt & sugar to taste

ULAM INGREDIENTS
100 g. bean sprouts (tailed)
3 turmeric leaves/ ⎱
 daun kunyit
1 stalk lemon grass/
 serai   thinly
½ cucumber   shredded
50 g. *daun selom*
2 stalks *daun kesum* ⎰

SAMBAL INGREDIENTS
4 tablespoons oil ⎱
10 dried chillies
 (sliced & soaked in
 hot water for   blended
 10 minutes)   to a
1 large onion   paste
4 shallots
2 cloves garlic ⎰
½ teaspoon ⎱ combined
 asam jawa ⎰ & strained
100 ml. water
60 ml. chilli sauce
salt & sugar to taste

1 Bring to the boil rice, water and *bunga talang* juice or blue colouring till the moisture is almost completely absorbed. Reduce heat, cover pan and leave till well cooked.

2 To prepare coconut *sambal*: Dry-fry the grated coconut till almost crispy and golden. Discard bones and head of mackerel; pound the flesh. Combine all the ingredients and season to taste.

3 To prepare *sambal*: Heat the oil; stir-fry the blended paste till fragrant. Add in *asam jawa* juice, chilli sauce, salt and sugar. Cook till the oil floats, then remove from heat.

4 Fluff rice with a fork. Add all the *ulam* ingredients. Serve *kerabu* rice with *budu*, fish crackers, salted eggs and sliced lime.

KUIH KOSUI

Serves 6-8

500 ml. water
80 g. palm sugar
80 g. brown sugar
80 g. granulated sugar
3 *pandan* leaves (knotted)
120 g. rice flour
60 g. tapioca flour
60 g. Hoen Kwee flour
250 ml. water
2 teaspoons slaked lime water/
   air kapur
200 g. grated coconut (reserve
   white part)
a pinch of salt

1 Combine 500 ml of water, palm sugar, brown sugar, granulated sugar and *pandan* leaves. Cook till sugar dissolves.

2 Remove syrup; leave to cool. Then discard *pandan* leaves.

3 Mix the syrup with rice flour, tapioca flour, Hoen Kwee flour, water and slaked lime water to a smooth batter.

4 Strain into a jug for easy pouring.

5 Grease small moulds with oil. Fill moulds with batter to almost four-fifths full.

6 Steam over high heat till set (the middle of *kuih* should sink in slightly). Remove from steamer and let *kuih* cool completely.

7 Add a pinch of salt to grated coconut. Turn out *kuih kosui* and serve with the grated coconut.

KUIH SERI MUKA

Serves 6-8

BOTTOM LAYER INGREDIENTS
420 g. glutinous rice/pulut
  (soaked overnight)
sufficient water
400 ml. coconut milk (from ½
  coconut)
½ teaspoon salt

TOP LAYER INGREDIENTS
2 eggs
100 g. granulated sugar
15 screwpine/ ⎱ blended &
pandan leaves ⎰ strained
200 ml. water
90 g. all-purpose flour
2 tablespoons cornflour
300 ml. coconut milk (from 1
  coconut)
a dash of green colouring
¼ teaspoon salt

1 **To prepare bottom layer:** Drain well the glutinous rice; put in a round 22 cm. tin. Mix coconut milk and salt. Slowly pour onto the rice.

2 Steam rice mixture over high heat till well-cooked. Press down with a banana leaf to ensure rice is evenly spread and very compact.

3 **To prepare top layer:** Beat eggs and sugar till the sugar dissolves. Combine well *pandan* juice, flour, cornflour, coconut milk, salt and green colouring to the egg mixture.

4 Strain onto the bottom layer. Return to steamer; cook for 25-30 minutes or till cooked.

5 Remove from heat; allow to cool. When completely cooled, slice *kuih seri muka* and serve.

SEAWEED JELLY

Serves 6-8

6 screwpine/
pandan leaves } blended &
200 ml. air   } strained
10 g. powdered *agar-agar*
600 ml. water
200 ml. thick coconut milk (from 1
  coconut)
80 g. granulated sugar
a dash of green colouring
2 eggs (lightly beaten)
¼ teaspoon salt

1 Combine *pandan* juice, *agar agar* powder, water, coconut milk, sugar and green colouring.

2 Stir till mixture is boiling and the sugar dissolves.

3 Add in eggs and salt; mix well and remove from heat.

4 Wet a 25 cm. pudding mould with water.

5 Gradually pour in the *agar agar* mixture and leave to set.

6 Refrigerate *agar-agar* for 1 hour. Slice the jelly and serve chilled.

BUBUR CHA CHA

Serves 4

- 100 g. assorted coloured *cha cha*
- 100 g. sweet potatoes (peeled & diced 1 cm.)
- 750 ml. coconut milk (from 1 coconut)
- 2 screwpine/pandan leaves (knotted)
- 50 g. palm sugar/gula melaka
- 30 – 35 g. granulated sugar
- ¼ teaspoon salt

1 Steam sweet potatoes till tender. Set aside.

2 Bring water to the boil. Add in *cha cha*; boil till tender. Remove.

3 Strain; shake under running tap water so that *cha cha* remain separated while cooling.

4 Combine coconut milk, *pandan* leaves, palm sugar, granulated sugar and salt. Stir over medium heat till boiling.

5 Tip in the *cha cha* and sweet potatoes. Simmer for 5 minutes.

6 Remove from heat. Dish up *cha cha* into individual bowls and serve hot.

BERGEDEL SAYUR (*Vegetable Patties*)

Serves 4

2 tablespoons oil
1 large onion ⎫
100 g. cabbage ⎬ finely chopped
150 g. carrots ⎭
80 g. green peas
1 teaspoon chilli powder
1 teaspoon fennel powder
300 g. potatoes (boiled, peeled & mashed)
4 stalks spring onion (chopped)
70-80 g. all-purpose flour
a little fresh milk (if needed)
150 g. breadcrumbs
salt to taste
oil for deep-frying

1 Sauté chopped onions, cabbage and carrots in hot oil till soft.

2 Mix in green peas, chilli powder and fennel powder. Stir for 1 minute.

3 Remove and transfer to a food processor. Combine mashed potatoes and chopped spring onions; process till a smooth texture.

4 Tip mixture into a bowl. Mix in flour and salt. Add in a little milk at a time if needed, till mixture holds together.

5 Shape mixture into balls and flatten slightly. Roll balls in breadcrumbs to cover completely.

6 Deep-fry balls in hot oil till patties turn golden brown. Remove from wok and drain well on paper towel before serving.

FRIED PANDAN CHICKEN

Serves 4

½ **chicken**
sufficient screwpine/pandan
   leaves (washed and drained)
oil for frying chicken
sufficient *lidi* **skewers**

MARINADE INGREDIENTS
2 stalks lemon grass/
   serai
100 g. galangal/
   lengkuas
100 g. turmeric/   } **blended**
   kunyit
100 g. garlic
100 g. shallots
2 eggs
a pinch of salt
1 teaspoon cornflour
1 teaspoon Worcestershire
   sauce

1 Wash chicken and pat dry with a towel. Cut into small pieces.

2 Mix chicken pieces with the marinade ingredients; set aside for 30 minutes.

3 Fold 2 *pandan* leaves to form a cone-shaped packet. Insert a piece of chicken and fold the leaves to form a triangular shape. Secure packet with a *lidi* skewer. Repeat the process until chicken pieces are finished.

4 Place the chicken packets in a steaming tray. Steam over medium heat for 10-15 minutes. Remove and drain.

5 Heat sufficient oil in a wok; fry the chicken packets over low heat for 10 minutes or until well-cooked.

6 Remove and drain well. Serve *pandan* chicken while still hot.

TELUR BUNGKUS DAGING (*Stuffed Eggs*)

Serves 4

4 tablespoons oil
5 cloves garlic (finely minced)
1 large onion (diced small)
1 cm. dried shrimp paste/
belacan
2 teaspoons chilli paste
2 tablespoons chilli
sauce
3 tablespoons tomato   } mixed
sauce
2 tablespoons *Hoi Sin*
sauce
200 g. minced meat
100 g. mixed vegetables
4 stalks coriander
leaves   } finely
3 stalks spring   chopped
onions
8 eggs (lightly beaten with a
pinch of salt)
sugar & salt to taste

3 Pour in the sauce mixture and minced meat. Stir occasionally till the meat is cooked.

6 Spoon some meat filling in the middle of the omelette.

1 Heat half of the oil. Sauté garlic and onions till fragrant.

4 Stir in mixed vegetables, coriander leaves and spring onions. Season to taste with salt and sugar; remove from heat. The mixture should be quite dry.

7 Fold the opposite sides of the omelette in.

2 Add in the dried shrimp paste and chilli paste; stir for 1 minute.

5 Heat the remaining oil and fry the egg into a large omelette.

8 Continue folding twice to form a square egg parcel. Remove from heat and serve hot.

ICE CREAM PUDDING

Serves 6-8

10 g. agar-agar powder
500 ml. water
300 ml. evaporated milk
100 g. palm sugar/gula melaka
4 tablespoons custard powder
1 teaspoon vanilla essence
2 eggs
100 ml. fruit syrup (from canned fruits)
200 ml. vanilla ice-cream
¼ teaspoon salt
canned fruits (for garnishing)

1 Stir *agar-agar* powder, water and evaporated milk over medium heat till the *agar-agar* dissolves.

2 Add in palm sugar; mix till boiling.

In a bowl, combine custard powder, vanilla essence, eggs and fruit syrup.

4 Strain egg mixture into milk mixture. Stir till mixture thickens. Remove.

5 Mix in the ice-cream and salt; combine well.

6 Wet a 1.2 litres pudding mould with water. Pour pudding mixture into the mould.

7 Allow mixture to set before refrigerating.

8 Turn out pudding onto a serving platter. Garnish with fruits; slice pudding and serve chilled.

MIXED FRIED SAMBAL

Serves 4

200 ml. oil
2 cakes bean curd (halved)
150 g. fermented soyabean cake/
   tempe (thinly sliced)
50 g. dried anchovies (cleaned &
   halved)
40 g. transparent vermicelli/suun
   (soaked till softened)
80 g. groundnuts
2 tablespoons chilli paste
50 ml. water
1-2 tablespoons thick *asam jawa*
   juice
½ teaspoon dark soya sauce
1 teaspoon sugar
salt to taste

BLENDED INGREDIENTS
5 shallots
2 cloves garlic
1 cm. dried shrimp paste/belacan

1 Heat 150 ml. oil; fry the bean curd till light brown. Remove and drain well. Then slice thinly.

2 Heat the oil again; fry the fermented soya bean cakes till golden brown. Remove and drain well on paper towel.

3 Dry-fry groundnuts till crispy (skins should be dark brown). Set aside.

4 Deep-fry the anchovies till crispy. Remove and drain well.

5 Heat the remaining 50 ml. oil; stir-fry blended paste, chilli paste and water till aromatic.

6 Mix in *asam jawa* juice, dark soya sauce, sugar and salt. Combine well.

7 Add in *suun*, bean curd, fermented soya bean cake and groundnuts. Mix thoroughly and cook till almost dry.

8 Season to taste, dish out onto a plate and serve.

SQUIDS IN SPICY SANTAN

Serves 4

600 g. squids (sliced crosswise and scalded)
300 g. *choy tam*
3 cloves garlic (peeled)
½ red capsicum } **cut into**
½ green capsicum } **wedges**
2 red chillies (finely sliced)
6 slices carrots
5 broccoli florets (cut small)
1 stalk celery (cut lengthwise)
1 stalk lemon grass/serai (bruised)
1 teaspoon turmeric/kunyit
1 teaspoon chopped shallots
1 teaspoon chopped garlic
3 slices ginger
2 tablespoons margarine
oil for frying

SEASONING INGREDIENTS
1 teaspoon chicken stock granules
80 ml. thick coconut milk/santan

1 Bring water to the boil; scald the *choy tam,* capsicum wedges, sliced red chillies and carrot for a short while. Remove and dip into cold water. Drain.

2 Heat oil and fry the chopped garlic until lightly browned. Remove from heat and put aside.

3 Heat margarine; sauté the lemon grass, turmeric, chopped shallots, garlic and sliced ginger until fragrant.

4 Add in scalded squids, fried garlic and scalded vegetables except *choy tam.* Stir to mix well over low heat.

5 Put in the seasoning ingredients and stir well.

6 Remove from heat when the dish is boiling.

7 Arrange the *choy tam* on a plate. Dish out the food onto the *choy tam.* Serve hot.

CHANG PARCELS

Serves 4

12 dried bamboo leaves/daun buluh kering
1 kg. glutinous rice/beras pulut
300 g. chicken (deboned and cut into 6 pieces)
6 dried chestnuts
6 dried black mushrooms ⎫ soaked
200 g. dried oysters ⎬ and drained
6 salted egg yolks
8 tablespoons oil
sufficient dry strings

SAUTÉING INGREDIENTS FOR RICE
200 g. garlic ⎫ chopped
200 g. shallots ⎭
2 teaspoons thick soya sauce
2 teaspoons light soya sauce
1 teaspoon five spice powder

SAUTÉING INGREDIENTS FOR CHICKEN
1 bulb garlic (chopped)
a pinch of five spice powder
a dash of pepper
1 tablespoon sesame oil
1 tablespoon oyster sauce
200 g. dried prawns (soaked)
100 g. dried cuttlefish (finely sliced)

1 Clean the dried bamboo leaves. Boil for 10 minutes. Remove and drain.

2 Wash the glutinous rice. Soak for 30 minutes. Remove and drain.

3 Boil the dried chestnuts for 10 minutes. Remove and dip into cold water. Discard the shells.

4 Heat 2 tablespoonfuls oil; fry glutinous rice over moderate heat. Add in the sautéing ingredients for the rice.

5 Mix thoroughly for 15 minutes while sprinkling 4 tablespoonfuls oil. Remove and set aside. Divide glutinous rice into 6 portions.

6 Heat 2 tablespoonfuls oil; sauté the chopped garlic until lightly browned. Put in the chicken pieces and sautéing

ingredients for chicken. Mix well. Remove from heat and set aside.

7 Fold 2 bamboo leaves to form a triangular shape. Put half of a portion of glutinous rice in the middle and spread evenly. Place a piece of chicken, a chestnut, a dried mushroom, an oyster and a salted egg yolk. Spread on top with the other half of the glutinous rice.

8 Cover the rice with the two ends of the bamboo leaves. Tie with a piece of dry string to prevent the filling from coming out. Repeat the process for the remaining ingredients.

9 Place *chang* in a steamer; steam for 2 hours. Transfer to a serving plate and serve hot.

PRAWN MEE

Serves 4

2 *l* water
1 kg. prawns (cleaned)
2 cm. dried shrimp paste/
   belacan (roasted and ground)
1 whole chicken bones (cleaned)
600 g. chicken breast
1 rock sugar
salt to taste
2 teaspoons seasoning powder
600 g. yellow noodles/mee
   (scalded and drained)
2 eggs (boiled, shelled and
   sliced)
200 g. bean sprouts (scalded
   and drained)
some fried shallots

SAUCE INGREDIENTS
125 ml. oil
1 tablespoon chopped shallots
1 tablespoon chopped garlic
300 g. dried chillies (soaked and
   finely chopped)
100 g. dried shrimp powder
2 cm. dried shrimp paste/
   belacan (roasted and ground)
1 tablespoon sugar

1 Boil the prawns in water. Remove and dip into cold water to cool prawns. Shell prawns and reserve the shells. Keep prawns aside.

2 Heat 1 tablespoonful oil. Sauté the dried shrimp paste and prawn shells until fragrant. Remove and pound until fine.

3 Add pounded prawns and chicken bones into the prawn stock. Simmer for 30 minutes.

4 Strain stock. Boil chicken breast until cooked. Remove, shred chicken and put aside.

5 Put in the rock sugar, salt and seasoning powder to the stock. Let it remain hot.

6 **To prepare sauce:** Heat oil. Sauté chopped shallots and garlic until lightly browned. Add in the remaining ingredients and combine well.

7 Arrange *mee* in a bowl and pour the gravy over noodles. Garnish with prawns, shredded chicken, sliced eggs, bean sprouts and fried shallots. Serve hot with the sauce.

VEGETABLE SOUP

Serves 4

3 tablespoons oil
2 cm. young ginger (finely shredded)
2 cloves garlic (finely minced)
100 g. chicken meat (diced)
100 g. medium-sized prawns
1 l chicken stock
1 large carrot (sliced)
100 g. mustard greens/sawi (cut 3 cm.)
100 g. cabbage (thickly sliced)
8 young corns (halved & cut 3 cm.)
100 g. button mushrooms (halved)
1 packet lily buds
1 packet transparent vermicelli/suun
3 stalks spring onion } finely
3 stalks Chinese celery } chopped
salt & white pepper powder to taste

1 Sauté ginger and minced garlic in hot oil till the aroma rises.

2 Add diced chicken; stir for 3 minutes.

3 Mix in prawns, chicken stock and carrots.

4 When the carrots are half-cooked, add mustard greens, cabbage and young corns. Stir till boiling.

5 Add in mushrooms, lily buds, transparent noodles, salt and white pepper. As soon as the noodles are soft, remove from heat.

6 Dish up, then sprinkle chopped spring onions and celery on top of soup. Serve hot.

LEMANG

Serves 8-10

2 kg. glutinous rice (washed,
   drained & soaked overnight)
4-4.5 *l* coconut milk (from 2
   coconuts)
salt to taste
young banana leaves
5-6 *lemang* bamboo

1 Separate banana leaves from its
middle stem. Make a slit along one
of the stems. Insert one end of
banana leaf into the slit and roll
loosely.

2 Place the stem in the bamboo.
Slowly and carefully slide it out,
leaving the leaves in the bamboo.

3 Mix coconut milk with salt.
Mixture should be slightly saltier
than usual.

4 Place rice in a large bowl. Pour
the coconut milk until it is the same
level as the rice. Soak for
30 minutes.

5 Spoon the rice into the bamboo
to a level of 10 centimetres below
the bamboo opening.

6 Pour in coconut milk to a level
of 5 centimetres above the rice.
Shake the bamboo slightly a few
times to ensure the coconut milk
mixes with the rice completely.

7 Cook over an open fire (place
bamboos leaning on iron rods) for
about 5-6 hours, turning the
bamboos regularly. In the early
stages, they should be placed at a
distance from the fire. Care must be
taken to ensure they do not get
burnt.

8 As soon as the *lemang* is almost
cooked, place the bamboos nearer
to the embers. When cooked, leave
to cool before breaking open the
bamboos and slicing the *lemang*.
Serve.

CURRY MEE

Serves 4

500 g. fresh yellow
  noodles/mee ⎫
300 g. bean sprouts ⎬ scalded
  (tailed) ⎭

1 kg. cockles/kerang (boiled &
  shelled)

2 cakes bean curd (fried &
  sliced)

4 eggs (hardboiled & halved)

4 stalks spring onion (thinly
  sliced)

3 limes (quartered)

3 red chillies (sliced) ⎫
2 tablespoons thin ⎪
  soya sauce ⎬ combined
½ teaspoon sugar ⎪ well
½ teaspoon vinegar ⎪
a little water ⎭

GRAVY INGREDIENTS

3 tablespoons oil

4 cm. cinnamon stick ⎫ dry
2 cloves ⎭ spices

1 stalk curry leaf/daun kari

6 shallots ⎫
3 cloves garlic ⎬ finely
1 large onion ⎭ blended

4 tablespoons curry powder
  (mixed with a little water to
  a paste)

400 g. chicken (cut into small
  pieces)

1.5-2 *l* coconut milk (from 2
  coconuts)

1 piece dried assam

2 fish cakes (thinly sliced)

10 *taufu pok* (optional)

150 g. fish balls (halved)

salt & sugar to taste

1 To prepare gravy: Heat oil; saute dry spices, blended paste and curry leaves till fragrant.

2 Add in curry paste; stir for 2 minutes. Then put in chicken pieces and stir till the oil rises.

3 Gradually, pour in coconut milk and add dried assam. Bring gravy to the boil, then simmer for 10 minutes.

4 Add fish cakes, *taufu pok* and fish balls. Leave to cook till the oil floats. Season to taste with salt and sugar.

5 Then, serve the noodles in small bowls topped with the garnishing ingredients. Ladle the hot curry onto the noodles before serving.

BUBUR KACANG HIJAU (*Green Mung Beans Porridge*)

Serves 4

200 g. green mung beans/ kacang hijau (washed)
sufficient water to cover beans
80 g, granulated sugar
50 g. palm sugar/gula melaka
2 screwpine/pandan leaves (knotted)
¼ teaspoon salt
750 ml. coconut milk (from 1 coconut)
3-4 pieces durian flesh (optional)

1 Boil green mung beans in water till almost tender.

2 Combine sugar, palm sugar, *pandan* leaves and salt. Stir occasionally till tender, adding a little water if necessary.

3 Gradually, pour in coconut milk and add in durian pieces. Cook mixture over medium heat.

4 When the porridge boils, remove from heat.

5 Dish out porridge into small bowls and serve hot.

MEE BANDUNG

Serves 4

500 g. topside beef (cut into
   3 pieces)
1.5 *l* water
300 g. medium-sized prawns
3 tablespoons oil
3 large tomatoes ⎱ finely
300 ml. water   ⎰ blended
1 tablespoon tomato puree
1.5 *l* water
250 g. mustard greens/sawi (cut
   3 cm.)
1 tablespoon flour ⎱ combined
200 ml. water   ⎰ well
4 eggs
500 g. yellow noodles/mee
5 stalks spring onion (thinly
   sliced)
3 limes (halved)
2 red chillies (thinly sliced)
fried shallots (for garnishing)
salt & sugar to taste

GROUND INGREDIENTS
1 large onion
4 cloves garlic
3 tablespoons dried shrimps
   (soaked)
1½ tablespoons chilli paste

1 Boil beef in water till tender. Remove beef, then boil prawns till cooked through. Remove and strain the stock. Slice the beef thinly. Set aside.

2 Heat oil and sauté the ground ingredients till fragrant.

3 Combine the blended tomatoes, tomato puree and stock.

4 Stir till boiling. Add in mustard greens and flour mixture. Season to taste with salt and sugar.

5 Break an egg at a time into the hot soup, stirring slowly till the eggs are almost cooked. Remove.

6 Divide noodles into individual bowls. Pour in the hot gravy, then garnish with sliced beef, prawns, spring onions, limes, red chillies and fried shallots. Serve hot.

AYAM MASAK MERAH

Serves 4-6

1 chicken (cut into 10 pieces)
1 tablespoon curry powder
½ teaspoon turmeric powder/
  serbuk kunyit
salt to taste
250 ml. oil
3 cloves ⎫
3 cardamoms ⎬ dry spices
5 cm. cinnamon stick ⎭
2 large onions ⎫
6 cloves garlic ⎬ blended to a paste
4 cm. ginger ⎭
2 tablespoons chilli paste
200 ml. tomato puree
400 ml. thick coconut milk (from 1
  coconut)
salt & sugar to taste

GROUND INGREDIENTS
1½ teaspoons fennel ⎫
  seeds ⎪
1 teaspoon cummin ⎬ dry-fried
  seeds ⎪
¼ teaspoon black ⎭
  peppercorn

1 Marinate chicken pieces with curry powder, turmeric powder and salt for 1 hour.

2 Heat oil; deep-fry chicken pieces till half-cooked. Remove from heat.

3 Remove half of the oil and sauté the dry spices for 1 minute.

4 Combine the blended paste; stir till fragrant.

5 Then mix in the ground spices, chilli paste and tomato puree. Pour in some water. Cook till the oil rises to the top.

6 Pour in coconut milk. Season to taste, then add chicken pieces.

7 Stir occasionally till the mixture boils and the gravy thickens. Dish up and serve.

KUIH LAPIS

Serves 4

500 g. rice flour
800 g. castor sugar
500 ml. cold water
500 ml. boiling water
**250 ml. thick coconut milk/
  santan**
**3 food colourings (assorted
  colours)**

1 Combine rice flour and sugar in a mixing bowl. Blend well. Gradually pour in cold water while stirring continuously. Stir until well-blended.

2 Pour boiling water into the mixture. Continue stirring until mixture is half-cooked. Pour in the thick coconut milk; stir until well-mixed.

3 Divide mixture into 3 portions. Colour each portion with a different food colouring.

4 Ladle out one portion of the mixture onto a steamer tray (having a thickness of 2 mm). Steam for 5 minutes. Remove from steamer.

5 Pour another portion with a different colouring, (about 2 mm thick) onto the steamed layer. Steam for a further 5 minutes. Remove.

6 Repeat step 5 with the third coloured mixture; steam for another 5 minutes.

7 Repeat the process until all the mixture is used up. Remove.

8 Cool the *kuih lapis* and cut to desired shapes before serving.

KUIH KOLE KACANG

Serves 6-8

- **100 g. brown sugar/gula merah**
- **200 g. granulated sugar**
- **200 ml. water**
- **200 g. green bean flour (dry-fried & cooled)**
- **400 ml. water**
- **500 ml. thick coconut milk (from 1 coconut)**
- **¼ teaspoon salt**
- **500 ml. thick coconut milk (for *tahi minyak*)**
- **oil to grease tin**

1 Bring to the boil brown sugar, granulated sugar and 200 ml. water till all the sugars have dissolved. Leave to cool.

2 Combine flour, water, thick coconut milk and salt till smooth. Strain into a wok.

3 Stir over low heat till mixture is thick and cooked.

4 Grease a square 22 cm. tin with oil. Pour the mixture on top, then flatten it with a banana leaf or the back of a spoon.

5 Leave to cool before slicing *kuih*.

6 **To prepare *tahi minyak*:** Stir thick coconut milk over low heat for 1 hour or till it turns to oil. The brownish residue that is formed is called *tahi minyak*.

7 Sprinkle the cooled *kuih* with *tahi minyak*, then cut into slices. This *kuih* may be served during tea.

THOSAI

Serves 6

200 g. black gram dhal
   (peeled)
360 g. rice flour
1 tablespoon salt
500-600 ml. water
40 g. ghee

1 Soak black dhal for 1 hour.

2 Blend dhal and salt with water till fine. Mix with rice flour and salt. Batter should not be too thick.

3 Leave batter overnight or for 8-10 hours. Refrigerate if not using immediately. Mix with some water to a thick but smooth batter.

4 Grease a flat pan with ghee. Gently, ladle some batter onto the centre of the pan; Smooth out into a big round with the back of a ladle in a circular motion.

5 When the underside is light brown, sprinkle ½ teaspoon ghee on top. Turn over *thosai* and cook the other side.

6 Remove from pan and serve *thosai* hot.

STUFFED SQUIDS

Serves 3-4

6 medium squids
100 g. glutinous rice/pulut
(soaked overnight)
100 g. chicken meat } **finely**
1 large onion } **minced**
1 red chilli (seeded & finely
chopped)
400 ml. coconut milk (from 1
coconut)
1 turmeric leaf/daun kunyit
½ teaspoon fenugreek/halba
1 shallot (finely minced)
salt & sugar to taste
6 cocktail sticks

3 Pull out the transparent cartilage.

6 Stuff the glutinous rice mixture into the squids until three-quarters full.

1 Pull out the squids' heads slowly.

4 Peel off the dark skin of the squids. Clean and set aside.

7 Stick the squids' tentacles onto the upper portion of the squids with cocktail sticks.

2 Cut off and discard the eyes and ink pouches.

5 Steam the glutinous rice and minced chicken for 15 minutes. Remove and place in a bowl. Tip in the chopped red chillies and minced onions. Season to taste with salt.

8 Boil stuffed squids with coconut milk, shallots, turmeric leaf, fenugreek, salt and sugar till quite thick. Remove from heat.

BRAISED CHICKEN WITH MUSHROOMS

Serves 4-6

1 chicken (cut into 10 pieces)
½ teaspoon salt
½ teaspoon black pepper powder
oil for sautéing
1 large onion } finely
4 cloves garlic } chopped
3 cm. ginger (finely shredded)
50 g. dried black mushrooms (soaked in hot water)*
1 teaspoon cornflour } thickening
3 tablespoons water } paste
2 red chillies (seeded & sliced lengthwise)
5 stalks spring onion (cut into 3 cm. lengths)
salt & sugar to taste

SAUCE INGREDIENTS
300 ml. stock from soaked mushrooms*
3 tablespoons oyster sauce
1 teaspoon thick soya sauce
2 teaspoons sweet soya sauce
2 tablespoons Hoi Sin sauce

1 Marinate chicken pieces, salt and black pepper powder for 30 minutes.

2 Heat oil; fry chicken pieces till half-cooked. Remove from heat. Leave aside.

3 Leave 3 tablespoonfuls oil in the wok. Sauté chopped onions, garlic and shredded ginger till fragrant.

4 Put in sauces, black mushrooms and chicken pieces. Cook till boiling. Reduce heat; simmer till the chicken is completely cooked.

5 Mix in the thickening paste. Season to taste; stir till mixture is quite thick.

6 Dish up into a casserole. Garnish with sliced red chillies and spring onions. Serve hot.

ACAR SAYUR CAMPUR *(Pickled Mixed Vegetables)*

Serves 4

400 g. groundnuts
200 g. sesame seeds (dry-fried)
50 g. dried chillies
  (soaked in hot
  water) } blended
100 g. turmeric/
  kunyit
250 g. long beans (cut lengthwise)
250 g. cucumber } cut into 2.5 cm
250 g. carrots } lengths and ½ cm thickness
250 g. cabbage (coarsely
  chopped)
1 large onion (thinly sliced)
2 tablespoons sour plum
  sauce
250 g. sugar

1 Fry the groundnuts without oil until fragrant. Discard the skins and pound. Put aside.

2 Bring water to the boil; scald the long beans, cucumber, carrots, chopped cabbage and sliced onion for a while. Remove and drain well.

3 In a mixing bowl, mix the pounded groundnuts, sesame seeds, dried chillies, turmeric, scalded vegetables, sour plum sauce and sugar until well-combined.

4 Allow vegetables to refrigerate for 30 minutes before serving.

CHICKEN SIEW PAU

Serves 4

1 kg. high protein flour
2 tablespoons margarine
2 teaspoons baking powder ⎤
2 tablespoons water ⎦ mixed thoroughly
2 tablespoons sugar
250 ml. water

FILLING INGREDIENTS
200 g. shallots ⎤ chopped
100 g. garlic ⎦
200 g. green peas
500 g. chicken breast (diced)
1 teaspoon sugar
1 teaspoon seasoning powder
1 tablespoon oyster sauce
3 tablespoons oil

FOR DECORATION
2 egg yolks
1 tablespoon maltose

1 Mix the high protein flour with the margarine. Add in baking powder, sugar and water. Knead until the mixture becomes a pliable dough. Put aside.

2 To prepare filling: Heat 3 tablespoonfuls oil. Sauté the chopped shallots and garlic until golden. Add in green peas, diced chicken, sugar, seasoning powder and oyster sauce. Cook over low heat until filling turns dry. Remove and leave to cool.

3 Heat the oven to 350°C.

4 Pinch some dough; roll out dough to form a flat, round shape. Put some filling in the centre. Meet the edges of dough in the centre; roll into a ball.

5 Arrange the finished dough on a baking tray.

6 To prepare decoration: Melt the maltose and mix thoroughly with the egg yolks. Brush tops of the dough with maltose mixture.

7 Bake for 45 minutes or until *pau* turns golden in colour. Remove from the oven and allow to cool before serving.

PENGAT PISANG (*Banana Porridge*)

Serves 4

6 ripe *pisang nangka*
300 ml. water
40 g. palm sugar/gula melaka
20 g. granulated sugar
1 screwpine/pandan leaf
 (knotted)
450 ml. coconut milk (from
 1 coconut)
a pinch of salt

1 Peel bananas and cut at a slant.

2 Combine bananas, water, palm sugar, sugar and *pandan* leaves in a pot.

3 Bring to the boil; stirring often till the liquid is reduced by half.

4 Pour in coconut milk and add salt. Stir till the porridge boils and coconut milk is well-cooked.

5 Remove from heat. Dish out and serve hot porridge in individual bowls.

Nasi Dagang – Gulai Ikan Tongkol

Serves 4-6

600 g. red glutinous unpolished rice (washed & soaked overnight)
250 ml. thick coconut milk ⎫ from 1
250 ml. thin coconut milk ⎬ coconut
3 shallots ⎫ thinly
1 cm. ginger ⎬ sliced
1 teaspoon fenugreek/halba
salt to taste

IKAN TONGKOL CURRY INGREDIENTS
600 g. *ikan tongkol* slices
1 dried assam slice
sufficient water (to cover rice)
3 tablespoons oil
10-12 dried chillies* ⎫
5 shallots ⎪ blended
1 clove garlic ⎬ to a
1 cm. galangal/lengkuas ⎭ paste
3 teaspoons coriander ⎫ dry-fried &
1 teaspoon fennel ⎬ blended
½ teaspoon turmeric powder
600 ml. coconut milk (from 1 coconut)
1 stalk lemon grass/serai (bruised)
1 tablespoon thick *asam jawa* juice
1 tablespoon *kerisik* (pounded crispy-fried grated coconut)
2 red chillies ⎫ halved, do
2 green chillies ⎬ not split
sugar & salt to taste

1 To prepare *dagang* rice: Drain glutinous rice well; steam for 30 minutes. Combine thin coconut milk with salt; mix with the steamed rice. Return to steamer and cook for a further 20 minutes.

2 Tip rice into a bowl. Mix rice thoroughly with the thick coconut milk, shallots, ginger and fenugreek. Steam again for 15 minutes or till rice is cooked through.

3 To prepare curry gravy: Boil *ikan tongkol* slices with dried assam slice till cooked.

4 In another pot, heat oil; sauté the blended paste and turmeric powder till fragrant.

5 Pour in thick coconut milk. Add lemon grass, *asam jawa* juice and *kerisik*. Stir till gravy is boiling.

6 When the oil floats, stir in *ikan tongkol* slices, red and green chillies. Season to taste, then simmer till gravy is quite thick and the oil rises.

7 Dish up and serve hot with *dagang* rice.

*Dried chillies need to be cut, seeded and soaked in hot water till soft.

LONTONG

Serves 6-8

420 g. rice (washed & drained)
1.5 *l* water

GRAVY INGREDIENTS
1.5 *l* coconut milk (from 2
coconuts)
8 shallots
4 cloves garlic ⎫
80 g. dried prawns ⎬ **blended**
1 cm. turmeric/ ⎭ **to a paste**
kunyit
2 stalks lemon grass/serai
(bruised)
1 dried assam slice
1 medium carrot ⎫
60 g. cabbage ⎪
1 long brinjal ⎬ **cut into**
80 g. fermented ⎪ **(3 x 1) cm.**
soya bean cake ⎭
6 long beans (cut 3 cm.)
3 soya bean skin/fu chok
(soaked till soft & cut 3 cm.)
30 g. transparent vermicelli/
suun (soaked till softened)
1 soya bean cake (fried &
thinly sliced)
salt to taste

1 **To prepare compressed rice:**
Boil rice in water till soft. Stir often
so that the rice does not stick to the
pot.

2 When the rice is very soft,
pound with a mortar. Tip into a
container, cover and press with a
heavy object. Allow rice to cool.
Then cut into cubes.

3 **To prepare gravy:** Stir in
coconut milk, blended paste, lemon
grass and assam slice till boiling.

4 Add the carrots; stir for
2 minutes. Then mix in the
cabbage, brinjal, fermented soya
bean cake, long beans, soya bean
skin, transparent noodles and soya
bean cake. Add salt to taste.

5 When the gravy boils again,
remove from heat. Dish up and
serve with the diced rice.

TIPS
If using instant pressed rice, boil with several *pandan* leaves so that the rice will
become more aromatic.

LAKSAM

Serves 4-6

LAKSAM INGREDIENTS
200 g. rice flour
40 g. all-purpose flour
¼ teaspoon salt
600 ml. water
oil (to grease tins)

GRAVY INGREDIENTS
500 g. mackerel/ikan kembung
(boiled, heads & bones
discarded, pounded)
2 l coconut milk (from 2
coconuts)
6 shallots ⎱
1 cm. ginger ⎰ **blended well**
1 piece dried assam
2 teaspoons black pepper
(ground)
salt to taste

ACCOMPANIMENTS
6 red chillies (blended to a
paste with some salt)
1 cucumber ⎱ **thinly**
10 long beans ⎰ **sliced**
40 g. *daun selom* (finely sliced)
200 g. bean sprouts (tailed)
3 cm. dried shrimp paste/
belacan (roasted & broken
into pieces)
3 limes (quartered)

1 Bring to the boil pounded fish, shallots mixture and dried assam; stirring often.

2 Add in black pepper powder and salt; reduce heat and simmer till the gravy thickens.

3 **To prepare *laksam*:** Combine rice flour, all-purpose flour, salt and water till a smooth batter is obtained.

4 Grease 2 or 3 tins measuring 22 cm. in diameter with oil. Ladle a thin layer of batter into each tin. Steam for 2-3 minutes or till set. Remove and roll while still hot. Repeat process till all the batter is used up.

5 Slice each roll to a thickness of 1 cm. Divide into small bowls.

6 Garnish with the accompaniments, then ladle hot gravy on top before serving.

AYAM PERCIK

Serves 4-6

1 chicken
1 *l* coconut milk (from 2
  coconuts)
2 tablespoons chilli paste
1 cm dried shrimp paste/
  belacan
1 teaspoon fenugreek/halba
2 slices dried assam
1 teaspoon sugar
salt to taste

BLENDED INGREDIENTS
8 shallots
2 cm. ginger
3 cm. turmeric/kunyit
2 cm. galangal/lengkuas
2 stalks lemon grass/serai

1 Score the breast and thighs of the chicken.

2 Bring to the boil coconut milk, chilli paste, dried shrimp paste, fenugreek, dried assam, sugar, salt and blended paste.

3 When the gravy boils, simmer till gravy reduces by half. Remove the assam.

4 Put in chicken, turning over a few times till it is almost cooked. Remove from heat.

5 Leave the gravy on very low heat.

6 Meanwhile, grill the chicken and baste with the gravy.

7 When the chicken is golden brown, dish up and serve with the thickened gravy.

CHICKEN SATAY

Serves 4-6

500 g. chicken meat
(cut 2 x 3 cm.)
bamboo skewers/satay sticks

BLENDED INGREDIENTS
2 shallots
1-2 tablespoons oil
2 cm. turmeric/kunyit
1 stalk lemon grass/serai
1 teaspoon sugar
1 teaspoon salt
2 teaspoons ⎫
  coriander ⎬ dry-fried
1 teaspoon ⎭
  cummin
¼ teaspoon cinnamon powder

GRAVY INGREDIENTS
2 tablespoons oil
6 shallots ⎫
3 cloves garlic ⎪
3 stalks lemon grass/ ⎪
  serai ⎬ blended
2 cm. galangal/ ⎪
  lengkuas ⎪
2 cm. ginger ⎭
1 teaspoon fennel ⎫ dry-fried
1 tablespoon ⎬ & ground
  coriander ⎭
3 tablespoons chilli paste
300 g. groundnuts (dry-fried,
  half ground & half pounded)
1 tablespoon *asam* ⎫ mixed &
200 ml. bone stock ⎭ strained
400 ml. coconut milk (from 1
  coconut)
2-3 tablespoons sugar
salt to taste

ACCOMPANIMENTS
compressed rice (diced)
large onions (cut into wedges)
cucumbers (sliced)

1 To prepare *satay*: Marinate chicken pieces with blended ingredients for 4 hours.

2 Thread 3-4 chicken pieces on each bamboo skewer. When all the meat has been used up, grill them. Baste with oil by dipping the bruised end of a lemon grass.

3 To prepare gravy: Heat oil; stir-fry the blended paste, ground spices and chilli paste till fragrant.

4 Mix groundnuts, *asam* juice, coconut milk, sugar and salt. Stir till gravy is boiling and thick. Serve with *satay*, compressed rice, onion wedges and cucumber slices.

ROTI CANAI

Serves 4-6

600 g. wheat flour
1 teaspoon salt
1 teaspoon sugar
2 eggs (lightly beaten)
125 ml. fresh milk
125 ml. water
225 g. ghee

1 Mix flour, salt and sugar.

2 Stir in beaten eggs and milk. Add in water, a little at a time. Combine well till mixture holds together.

3 Knead dough for 10 minutes or till it is smooth and pliable. If too hard, wet palms with some water and continue kneading.

4 Divide dough into 7 or 8 balls. Coat with some oil and ghee. Place in a bowl; cover balls with a damp tea towel.

5 Leave dough balls for 6 hours or overnight.

6 Flatten balls with a rolling pin or palm into a thin circle. Gently pull the edges to a very thin pancake. Fold in both sides, then lift up one end. Coil to make a round shape.

7 Flatten dough again into a 20 cm. circle. Grease a flat pan with ghee and fry the pancake.

8 Turn over pancake and fry the other side. Both sides should be golden brown and crisp. Remove from pan and serve immediately.

9 Repeat the process untill dough is all used up.

SZECHUAN TOFU

Serves 4

3 pieces tofu (diced)
300 g chicken
300 g beef } minced
3 teaspoons garlic
4 dried black mushrooms
(soaked and finely sliced)
3 tablespoons spring onions
(finely chopped)
a few red chillies (cut into
small pieces)
3 tablespoons oil for sautéing

SEASONING INGREDIENTS
1½ teaspoons sesame oil
1½ teaspoons chilli powder
1½ tablespoons oyster sauce
1½ teaspoons chicken stock
granules
1½ teaspoons broad bean
paste

1 Heat oil in a wok. Sauté minced meat until well-cooked.

2 Add in the minced garlic and black mushrooms. Fry for about 1 minute.

3 Add in diced tofu and the seasoning ingredients. Stir slowly and leave to boil. Then reduce heat and leave for about 5-10 minutes.

4 Remove from heat. Sprinkle chopped spring onions and red chillies on top of tofu. Serve hot with boiled, white rice.

STUFFED FRIED CENCARU

Serves 4

4 *cencaru* fish (slit lengthwise
through the back)
¼ teaspoon turmeric powder/
serbuk kunyit
oil for deep-frying
salt & sugar to taste

BLENDED INGREDIENTS
2 red chillies
1 tablespoon chilli paste
3 shallots
2 cloves garlic
1 stalk lemon grass/serai
1 cm. dried shrimp paste/belacan
1 tablespoon *asam jawa* juice
60 g. grated coconut

1 Rub fish with turmeric powder and salt. Set aside for 20 minutes.

2 Add salt and sugar to the blended paste.

3 Stuff the paste into the fish cavity.

4 Heat oil; deep-fry fish till cooked. Turn over fish and cook the other side.

5 Remove from heat and drain well. Serve hot.

MALAY-STYLE ROJAK

Serves 4-6

200 g. bean sprouts (tailed &
  blanched)
200 g. yam bean/sengkuang
  (peeled & sliced)
200 g. cucumber (sliced)
3 cakes bean curd (fried &
  thinly sliced)
4 eggs (hardboiled, shelled &
  sliced)

PRAWN FRITTERS
INGREDIENTS
100 g. all-purpose flour
20 g. rice flour
200 g. medium-sized prawns
  (peeled)
1 egg
1 green chilli ⎫ seeded &
1 red chilli ⎭ finely chopped
15 stalks chives (finely
  chopped)
a little water
salt to taste
oil for frying

GRAVY INGREDIENTS
3 tablespoons oil
8 shallots ⎫ finely
4 cloves garlic ⎭ blended
2-3 tablespoons chilli paste
200 g. sweet potatoes (peeled,
  boiled & mashed)
1 tablespoon *asam* ⎫ mixed &
  jawa   ⎬ strained
500 ml. water ⎭
2 tablespoons brown sugar/
  gula merah
200 g. groundnuts (dry-fried,
  skinned & ground)
salt to taste

1 **To prepare prawn fritters:**
Combine both flours and salt.

2 Mix in prawns, egg, chopped
chillies, chives and water to
obtain a smooth batter.

3 Heat oil; spoon batter into
hot oil and fry till golden brown.
Remove, drain well and slice
prawn fritters thinly.

4 **To prepare gravy:** Sauté
blended paste and chilli paste
till fragrant.

5 Combine the sweet potatoes,
asam jawa juice, sugar and salt.
Stir till gravy is boiling; simmer
for 30 minutes. Add water if
gravy is too thick.

6 Put in the groundnuts. Stir
until the mixture boils; remove
from heat.

7 Ladle the gravy over the
assorted vegetables, prawn
fritters, sliced bean curd and
hardboiled eggs to serve *rojak*.

GRILLED FISH

Serves 4

4 mackerel/ikan kembung
300 ml. coconut milk (from 1 coconut)
2-3 tablespoons chilli paste
1 slice dried *asam*
salt & sugar to taste

BLENDED INGREDIENTS
4 shallots
2 cloves garlic
½ cm. galangal/lengkuas
1 stalk lemon grass/serai

1 Season fish with a pinch of salt.

2 Arrange fish under a grill. Alternatively, pierce fish with bamboo skewer and place on a barbecue.

3 **To prepare sauce:** Bring to the boil blended paste, coconut milk, chilli paste, dried *asam,* salt and sugar. Simmer till sauce thickens.

4 Grill fish till half-cooked. Baste with the coconut sauce.

5 Repeat the process of grilling and basting until the fish is cooked.

6 Remove from grill and serve hot with the remaining sauce.

BUAH MELAKA

Serves 4-6

- 8 screwpine/pandan leaves ⎫
- 230 ml. water ⎬ blended & strained
- a dash of green colouring
- 250 g. glutinous rice flour/ tepung pulut
- 1 tablespoon all-purpose flour
- 1 tablespoon slaked lime water/*air kapur*
- 2-3 tablespoons water (optional)
- 120 g. palm sugar/gula melaka (diced)
- 200 g. grated coconut (reserve white part)
- a pinch of salt

2 Stir in the *pandan* juice. Knead lightly to make a soft dough, adding some water if necessary.

5 Bring water to the boil. Drop balls into the water.

1 Add all-purpose flour and slaked lime water into the glutinous rice flour. Mix thoroughly.

3 Shape dough into small balls. Flatten slightly; place a piece of palm sugar in the centre.

6 Cook until they float up. Drain well.

4 Roll up dough to enclose filling. Roll gently into a ball and set aside. Repeat this process until all the dough and palm sugar are used up.

7 Roll at once in the grated coconut mixed with the salt. Arrange on serving platter. Leave to cool, then serve.

TIPS
The grated coconut should be lightly steamed so that it will last longer and not turn rancid.

IKAN PARI MASAK ASAM PEDAS

Serves 4

500 g. stingray/ikan pari (cut into pieces)
3 tablespoons oil
sufficient water
5 sprigs polygonum leaves/daun kesum
1 stalk lemon grass/serai (bruised)
1 tablespoon *asam jawa* ⎫ mixed &
120 ml. water ⎭ strained
salt & sugar to taste

BLENDED INGREDIENTS
6 shallots
3 cloves garlic
½ cm. ginger
1 cm. dried shrimp paste/belacan
3-4 tablespoons chilli paste

1 Heat oil; sauté blended ingredients till fragrant.

2 Combine water, *daun kesum*, lemon grass, *asam* juice, salt and sugar.

3 Cook; stirring occasionally till gravy boils.

4 Add in *ikan pari* pieces; continue cooking over medium heat.

5 When the gravy boils and fish pieces are cooked, dish up into a casserole. Serve hot.

PUCUK UBI MASAK TEMPOYAK

Serves 6

100 g. tapioca shoots
10 pieces *daun kaduk* shoots ⎫
5 long beans   ⎬ thinly sliced
2 stalks lemon grass/serai ⎪
4 green chillies   ⎭

15 bird's eye chillies/ cili padi ⎫ pounded/ blended
1 cm. turmeric/kunyit ⎭

25 pieces *petai* (halved)
2-3 tablespoons *tempoyak*
40 g. dried anchovies (cleaned)
500 ml. coconut milk (from 1 coconut)
salt & sugar to taste

1 Combine the sliced vegetables, blended paste, *petai*, *tempoyak* and anchovies in a large pot.

2 Gradually pour in the coconut milk (add more water if needed), till the contents of the pot is immersed in liquid.

3 Bring to the boil; stirring continuously.

4 Adjust seasoning; continue stirring till all the vegetables are cooked.

5 Remove from heat and serve hot.

CHICKEN WITH YOUNG GINGER

Serves 4

600 g. chicken breast
400 g. young ginger (sliced)
100 g. garlic (chopped)
2 tablespoons oil

SEASONING INGREDIENTS
1 tablespoon oyster sauce
2 tablespoons fish gravy

1 Clean the chicken breasts and pat dry with a towel. Cut into long strips.

2 Heat oil. Sauté sliced ginger and chopped garlic until fragrant.

3 Put in the chicken strips and fry over moderate heat. Stir till mixed evenly.

4 Add in the seasoning ingredients and mix well.

5 Remove when cooked. Serve hot.

YAM IN ASSAM GRAVY

Serves 4-6

400 g. yam stalks (skinned & cut 2.5 cm)
600-700 ml. water
1 tablespoon *asam jawa* ⎫ **mixed & strained**
100 ml. water ⎭
3 tablespoons fish sauce
salt & sugar to taste

BLENDED INGREDIENTS
40 g. dried prawns ⎫ **soaked till soft**
15-20 dried chillies (seeded) ⎭
1.5 cm. turmeric/kunyit
2 cloves garlic
1 cm. dried shrimp paste/ belacan

1 Bring to the boil blended ingredients, water and yam stalks until half tender.

2 When boiling, reduce heat and simmer for 10-15 minutes or till tender.

3 Add in the *asam jawa* juice and fish sauce. Leave to boil. Adjust seasoning to taste.

4 Simmer for about 5 minutes and remove from heat.

5 Serve hot if preferred.

TIPS
If you wish to add yam to the dish, wash the yam after peeling, only then grate it. This will reduce the slime.

CURRY PUFFS

Serves 6-8

FILLING INGREDIENTS
2 tablespoons oil
1 large onion (finely chopped)
200 g. minced meat
1 stalk curry leaves/daun kari
3 tablespoons meat curry powder
a little water
300 g. potatoes (diced & boiled)
6 stalks celery (finely chopped)
salt & sugar to taste

PASTRY INGREDIENTS
500 g. all-purpose flour } **sifted**
¼ teaspoon salt
170 g. margarine
a little water
oil for deep-frying

1 To prepare filling: Heat oil; sauté chopped onions till fragrant. Add minced meat; stir for 3 minutes. Mix in curry leaves, curry powder and water, stirring till the meat is cooked. Put in the diced potatoes and chopped celery. Adjust seasoning; stir thoroughly, then remove. Leave to cool.

2 To prepare pastry: Rub margarine into the flour till mixture resembles breadcrumbs. Gradually add water and mix till pastry holds together. Knead lightly till smooth.

3 Roll out dough on a lightly floured board to a 5 mm. thickness. Cut into 9 cm. circles.

4 Place a tablespoon of filling in the centre of each circle; fold pastry over. Seal and flute the edges.

5 Heat oil for deep-frying. Fry curry puffs till golden brown. Drain well.

6 Dish up onto a serving plate. Serve warm or when cool.

TIPS
Fry the curry puffs first in medium-hot oil, then only increase the heat. This will avoid bubbling on the skin while frying.

MUTTON SOUP

Serves 6

- **1 kg. mutton with bones (cut small)**
- **1 tablespoon ginger juice**
- **½ teaspoon turmeric powder/ serbuk kunyit**
- **a pinch of salt**
- **3 tablespoons oil**
- **5 shallots (finely chopped)**
- **3-4 *l* water**
- **1 packet soup spices (tied in muslin)**
- **2 tablespoons thin soya sauce**
- **2 tablespoons sweet soya sauce**
- **½ teaspoon sugar**
- **4 tablespoons ground cashew nuts**
- **1 teaspoon rice flour }** mixed
- **120 ml. water**
- **3 stalks spring onion (finely chopped)**
- **8 shallots }** finely sliced & fried crisp
- **3 cloves garlic }**

SPICE INGREDIENTS
- **2 tablespoons coriander powder**
- **½ tablespoon fennel powder**
- **½ tablespoon cummin powder**

1 Marinate mutton pieces with ginger juice, turmeric powder and salt for 30 minutes.

2 Heat oil in a wok; sauté chopped shallots for ½ minute. Add spice ingredients and mutton pieces. Stir for 5 minutes.

3 Gradually pour in water, soup spices, thin soya sauce and sweet soya sauce. Adjust seasoning. Bring to the boil; simmer till the mutton is tender.

4 Add ground cashew nuts and rice flour mixture. Simmer and stir for about 5 minutes.

5 Remove and ladle soup into small bowls. Sprinkle with chopped spring onions, fried shallots and garlic.

TIPS

To reduce the oil in the soup, leave overnight or refrigerate briefly (after the soup has cooled). Then get rid of the fat which has solidified on the surface.

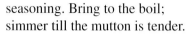

MASALA VADEI

Serves 6-8

300 g. yellow dhal (skinned)
45 g. rice flour
30 g. all-purpose flour
¾ teaspoon salt
1 teaspoon sugar
2 medium onions } finely
2 green chillies (seeded) } diced
1 tablespoon meat curry
  powder
oil for deep-frying

1 Soak dhal in hot water for 2 hours.

2 Strain water; blend in a food processor till very fine. If preferred, reserve a quarter of it unprocessed.

3 Combine dhal (including the unprocessed), rice flour, flour, salt, sugar, diced onions, green chillies and curry powder.

4 Pinch a portion of the mixture. Shape into round patties about 5 cm. in diameter. The middle part should be about 2 cm. thick.

5 Heat oil. Deep-fry *vadei* till golden brown.

6 Remove from wok. Drain well on paper towel and serve hot.

LENG CHEE KANG

Serves 4

600 g white lotus seeds/biji
  teratai putih
½ teaspoon slaked lime
  water/air kapur
2 *l* water
200 g. sago pearls (soaked and
  drained)
2 screwpine/pandan leaves
sufficient dried *longans*
  (washed)
500 g rock sugar

1 Wash the lotus seeds and soak overnight. Discard the young leaves from centres of lotus seeds.

2 Boil some water; add in the lotus seeds and slaked lime. Boil over moderate heat for 30-40 minutes. Remove lotus seeds and drain.

3 Bring 2 litres of water to the boil. Add lotus seeds, sago pearls and screwpine leaves. Simmer over low heat until the lotus seeds become soft.

4 Add in the dried *longans* and rock sugar. Leave to boil for a further 10-15 minutes. Remove from heat and cool before serving.

PAKORAS

Serves 4

- 125 g. chick peas flour/tepung kacang kuda
- 1 teaspoon salt
- ½ teaspoon chilli powder
- 160-180 ml. water
- 2 green chillies (seeded & finely chopped)
- 6 sprigs coriander leaves (finely shredded)
- 1 teaspoon ghee
- 200 g. potatoes } diced ½ cm.
- 1 large onion
- oil for frying

1 Combine flour, salt and chilli powder in a large bowl.

2 Mix in water, a little at a time; stirring until a thick batter.

3 Cover bowl and keep batter aside for 30 minutes.

4 Put in chopped green chillies, coriander leaves, ghee, diced potatoes and onions. Mix thoroughly.

5 Heat oil over medium heat. Drop tablespoonfuls of batter into hot oil.

6 Turn over batter and cook till golden brown.

7 Remove from heat; drain well. Dish out onto a serving plate and serve hot.

MASALA MACHI

Serves 4

4 mackerel/ikan kembung
  (scored)
salt to taste
a little water
2 tablespoons lime juice
2 cloves garlic
4 green chillies (seeded)
10 sprigs coriander leaves/
  daun ketumbar
1 teaspoon coriander powder
3 tablespoons oil
1 medium onion (finely
  chopped)

1 Rub mackerel with a pinch of salt. Leave aside.

2 With some water blend lime juice, garlic, green chillies, coriander leaves, coriander powder and salt to a paste.

3 Heat 2 tablespoons oil; sauté chopped onions till golden.

4 Add blended paste; fry over low heat till fragrant.

5 Remove and stuff paste into the fish cavity. Drizzle the remaining oil over the fish.

6 Grill or roast fish till cooked. If preferred, wrap fish in an aluminium foil. Bake at 180°C for 20-25 minutes.

7 Remove from grill. Transfer to a serving platter.

CHICKEN KAMPUNG-STYLE

Serves 4-6

1 chicken (cut into 10 pieces)
3 tablespoons oil
1 stalk lemon grass/serai (bruised)
800 ml. coconut
  milk } from 1
150 ml. thick } coconut
  coconut milk
3 potatoes (peeled & quartered)
1 slice dried *asam*
2 turmeric leaves/daun kunyit
  (finely sliced)
salt & sugar to taste

BLENDED INGREDIENTS
2 green chillies
1 red chilli
8-10 bird's eye chillies/cili padi
½ large onion
5 shallots
3 cloves garlic
2 cm. ginger
2 cm. turmeric/kunyit
1 stalk lemon grass/serai

1 Sauté the blended paste in hot oil till the oil floats.

2 Add the chicken pieces. Stir-fry for 2-3 minutes or till chicken juices begin to dry up.

3 Put in lemon grass, thin coconut milk, potatoes and dried *asam*. Season to taste with salt and sugar.

4 Stir occasionally till the potatoes are soft. Gradually pour in thick coconut milk and add turmeric leaves.

5 Return to the boil, then remove from heat. Serve hot.

KETUPAT *(Compressed Rice in Coconut Leaves)*

Serves 4-6

300 g. rice (washed & drained)
**15-20 *ketupat* parcels (made
from young coconut leaves)**
sufficient water (to boil rice)

1 Put rice into *ketupat* parcels to about one-third full.

2 Pull end part of leaves to ensure the parcels are intact.

3 Tie together six ends of parcels (or ten if making in large quantities) for easy handling.

4 Bring water to the boil in a large pot.

5 Place the parcels in the pot. Cook for 3-4 hours, stirring occasionally till the rice is packed and filled the parcels completely. Add more water if necessary.

6 As soon as parcels are cooked, remove from pot; hang the *ketupat* to let the excess water drip.

DRY CHICKEN CURRY

Serves 4-6

1 chicken (cut into 8 pieces)
80 ml. oil
10 shallots ⎤ blended or
2 cloves garlic ⎦ pounded
4 cm. cinnamon stick
1 star anise
3 cardamoms (bruised)
600 ml. thin coconut ⎤
  milk   ⎬ from 1
125 ml. thick coconut ⎥ coconut
  milk   ⎦
3 potatoes (quartered)
2 large onions (diced 1 cm.)
1-2 tablespoons lime juice
salt & sugar to taste

BLENDED INGREDIENTS
10-15 dried chillies
  (soaked till softened)
4 red chillies
2½ cm. turmeric/kunyit
1 stalk lemon grass/   ⎤ mixed
  serai   ⎬ to a
1½ cm. galangal/lengkuas ⎥ paste
1 cm. ginger
3 tablespoons *kerisik*
¼ teaspoon nutmeg
  powder

GROUND INGREDIENTS
4 tablespoons
  coriander   ⎤
1 tablespoon fennel ⎬ dry-fried
1 tablespoon cummin ⎥
1 tablespoon rice   ⎦
10 white peppercorns/lada putih
10 black peppercorns/lada hitam

1 Heat oil; sauté blended shallots and garlic till golden.

2 Add in blended ingredients and ground spices; stir till fragrant. Mix in cinnamon stick, star anise and cardamoms.

3 Stir-fry for 1 minute; put in chicken pieces. Gradually pour in 125 ml. thin coconut milk. Stir for 5 minutes.

4 Adjust seasoning and mix in the remaining thin coconut milk. Bring to the boil; simmer for 15 minutes and put in potatoes.

5 Stir occasionally until potatoes are soft; add in thick coconut milk, diced onions and lime juice.

6 When curry boils again, remove from heat. Dish up into a casserole and serve hot.

NASI ULAM

Serves 4

350 g. rice (washed & drained)
650 ml. water
1 teaspoon salt
2 tablespoons oil
50 g. salted *ikan kurau*
30 g. dried shrimps (soaked till softened)
4 tablespoons grated coconut (dry-fried till golden)
salt & black pepper powder to taste

ULAM INGREDIENTS
6 shallots
2 turmeric leaves/ daun kunyit
10 *kaduk* leaves
10 sprigs *pegaga* leaves   finely shredded
10 sprigs *ulam raja* leaves
10 sprigs *selom* leaves
1 stalk lemon grass/ serai

1 Bring to the boil rice in water. Add salt.

2 When almost all the moisture has been absorbed, cover pot and reduce heat. Cook for 8-10 minutes or till cooked through. Tip onto a large plate to cool and fluff rice with a fork.

3 Heat oil and fry the salted fish. Remove from wok, then pound or blend with dried shrimps till fine.

4 Combine all the *ulam* ingredients with the salted fish mixture, grated coconut, black pepper powder and rice.

5 Season with salt, if necessary. Serve immediately.

DENDENG DAGING

Serves 6

1 kg. beef (cut into large thin pieces)
50 g. cummin ⎱ **dry-fried &**
30 g. black pepper ⎰ **ground**
1 tablespoon lime juice
100 ml. oil
1 large onion ⎫
8 cloves garlic ⎬ **blended to**
3 shallots ⎪ **a paste**
4 red chillies ⎭
sufficient water
2 turmeric leaves/daun kunyit (finely shredded)
30 g. palm sugar/gula melaka
salt to taste

1 Marinate beef pieces with the ground spices and lime juice for 1 hour.

2 Heat half of the oil; sauté the blended paste till fragrant.

3 Add the beef pieces and stir till almost dry.

4 Mix in the water. Stir till the beef pieces are tender.

5 Put in the remaining oil, mix well and bring to the boil.

6 Add in the turmeric leaves, palm sugar and salt. Stir till the gravy is quite thick and oily. Remove from heat and serve.

RENDANG TOK

Serves 4-6

600 g. tender-cut beef (cut into 15 pieces)
3 tablespoons brown sugar/ gula merah
1 tablespoon *asam* ⎱ mixed &
100 ml. water ⎰ strained
1.5 *l* coconut milk (from 2 coconuts)
3 tablespoons oil
150 g. grated coconut (dry-fried till crisp; pounded to make *kerisik*)
salt to taste

BLENDED INGREDIENTS
3 tablespoons coriander ⎱ dry-
2 tablespoons fennel ⎰ fried
1 tablespoon cummin
1 teaspoon black pepper
15-20 dried chillies (soaked till softened)
4 stalks lemon grass/serai
4 cm. ginger
2.5 cm. galangal/lengkuas
2 large onions
3 candlenuts/buah keras

SAUTÉING INGREDIENTS
4 cloves garlic ⎱ thinly sliced
4 shallots ⎰
3 cm. cinnamon stick
4 cloves
3 cardamoms

1 Marinate beef pieces with blended ingredients, brown sugar, *asam jawa* juice, a little coconut milk and salt for 2 hours.

2 Heat oil; stir-fry sautéing ingredients till aromatic.

3 Add in beef pieces and stir-fry for about 15 minutes or till water has dried up.

4 Gradually pour in the coconut milk. Stir and cook till the gravy is reduced by half. Season to taste.

5 Mix in the *kerisik*. Stir often over low heat. When the gravy is very thick, dark brown in colour and oily, it is ready to be served.

6 Dish out onto a serving platter and serve hot.

TIPS
This dish must be cooked over a slow fire. It takes around 2½ hours to prepare.

KUBIS MASAK LEMAK *(Cabbage in Coconut Milk)*

Serves 4

400 g. cabbage (coarsely cut)
500 ml. thin coconut
  milk ⎫
          from ½
100 ml. thick coconut ⎬ **coconut**
  milk ⎭
4 shallots (thinly sliced)
150 g. shelled prawns
2 red chillies (cut at a slant)
salt to taste

1 Combine thin coconut milk, shallots and prawns. Bring to the boil; stirring continuously.

2 Add in the cabbage, thick coconut milk and salt.

3 Mix well and stir till the cabbage is soft.

4 Put in the sliced red chillies. Stir for 1 minute

5 Dish up into a casserole and serve hot.

FRIED KANGKUNG WITH BELACAN

Serves 4

2 cm. dried shrimp paste/
belacan (roasted and
pounded)
200 g. dried shrimps granules
some bird's eye chillies/cili
padi (bruised)
1 teaspoon chopped garlic
1 teaspoon chopped shallots
1 kg. water convolvulus/
kangkung (cut lengthwise)
1 teaspoon seasoning powder
3 tablespoons oil

1 Heat the oil; sauté chopped garlic and shallots until browned slightly.

2 Add in the dried shrimp paste, dried shrimps granules and bird's eye chillies. Stir-fry until well-mixed.

3 Add in the *kangkung* and stir-fry over high heat.

4 Sprinkle with the seasoning powder; remove when vegetables are cooked.

5 Dish out onto a plate. Serve while still hot.

PUTU MAYAM (*String-Hoppers*)

Serves 6-8

450 g. rice flour
250 ml. hot water
salt to taste

1 Dry-fry rice flour over low heat for 10 minutes.

2 Remove and place rice flour in a large bowl.

3 Add salt and hot water; stirring well to combine mixture.

4 Place dough into a string-hopper mould.

5 Press onto a wet muslin cloth or banana leaf.

6 Steam for 5-7 minutes or till cooked.

7 Remove from steamer. Serve string hoppers with *dalca*, curry or grated coconut mixed with some brown sugar.

PULUT INTI *(Glutinous Rice with Coconut)*

Serves 6-8

FILLING INGREDIENTS
100 g. palm sugar/gula melaka
100 ml. water
2 screwpine/pandan leaves
   (knotted)
120 g. grated coconut (reserve
   white part)
1 teaspoon all-purpose
   flour   } mixed
4 tablespoons water   } well

GLUTINOUS RICE INGREDIENTS
500 g. glutinous rice/pulut
   (soaked overnight)
2 screwpine/pandan leaves (cut
   into 4 cm. lengths)
250 ml. thick coconut milk (from 1
   coconut)
a pinch of salt
a few banana leaves
   (12 x 12 cm, scalded)

1 **To prepare filling:** Put palm sugar, water and *pandan* leaves in a large pan. Stir till sugar dissolves. Add in grated coconut and combine well; add some water if too thick. When almost done, mix in the flour mixture; stir to combine completely. Then remove and leave to cool.

2 **To prepare rice:** Steam glutinous rice with *pandan* leaves for 20 minutes or till almost cooked.

3 Add salt to thick coconut milk.

4 Transfer the rice into a big bowl. Stir in the coconut milk. Return to the steamer and cook for 15 minutes.

5 Place a spoonful of rice onto each banana leaf. Top rice with the coconut filling.

6 Wrap in a neat rectangular parcel. (The top part of the filling may be seen slightly). Serve.

PENANG FRIED KUEY TEOW

Serves 4

300 g. flat rice noodles/kuey teow
1 teaspoon garlic (chopped)
100 g. prawns (shelled and
   de-veined)
100 g. cockles (boiled and shelled)
200 g. bean sprouts (tailed)
some *kucai* leaves (cut
   lengthwise)
2 stalks mustard greens/sawi (cut
   lengthwise)
1 egg
1 tablespoon oil

SEASONING INGREDIENTS
1 teaspoon oyster sauce
½ teaspoon fish sauce
½ teaspoon light soya sauce
a pinch of seasoning powder

1 Heat oil in a wok and sauté chopped garlic until browned slightly.

2 Put in prawns and fry over high heat. Then, add in the *kuey teow*; mix well for 1 minute.

3 Add in cockles, bean sprouts, mustard greens and *kucai* leaves. Cook over moderate heat for 3-5 minutes. Add in the seasoning ingredients and mix thoroughly.

4 Push aside *kuey teow*. Break egg in the middle of the wok and fry until cooked. Mix the egg and *kuey teow* well.

5 Dish out onto a plate and serve hot.

CHICKEN KUT TEH

Serves 4

HERB INGREDIENTS
RM2 *yong sham su qiji*
yit di
tong sham
cummin seeds
fennel seeds
cinnamon peel
liquorice

} RM5 quantity

1 whole chicken
bones of a whole chicken
2 *l* water
6 bulbs garlic (washed)
4 dried black mushrooms
  (soaked and quartered)

SEASONING INGREDIENTS
100 ml. light soya sauce
salt to taste

1 Wash all the herbs. Clean the chicken and the bones.

2 Boil water and put in the chicken bones. Simmer for 1 hour. Strain the stock.

3 Add in the herbs, chicken, garlic, black mushrooms and the seasoning ingredients. Simmer approximately for 1 hour over moderate heat or until cooked.

4 Remove from stove. Remove the chicken and cut into pieces.

5 Serve hot with the soup.

SAYUR CEKUR BERKELEDEK

Serves 3-4

1 horse mackerel/ikan kembung
500 g. sweet potatoes (peeled & diced)
sufficient water
150 g. *daun cekur manis* (hard stalks discarded)
6 shallots
10 black peppercorns/lada hitam
salt & sugar to taste

1 Rub fish with salt and grill till well-cooked.

2 Discard bones and head of fish; pound flesh with shallots and black pepper.

3 Combine pounded ingredients, sweet potatoes, water, salt and sugar.

4 Bring to the boil; stirring occasionally.

5 When the potatoes are almost tender, add in the *daun cekur manis*. Stir till boiling and the *daun cekur* is soft.

6 Dish up and serve with boiled white rice.

ULAM DENGAN CICAH *(Vegetables with Dip)*

Serves 4-6

ASSORTED VEGETABLES

long beans (cut 2 cm.)
kangkung (cut 3 cm.)
long/round brinjals
  (cut according to   ⎱ blanched
  preference)
ladies' fingers
cabbage ⎱ coarsely cut
cucumber
petai (peeled)
four angled-beans/kacang botol
daun kaduk, daun selom, daun
  ulam raja, etc.

DIP INGREDIENTS

200 g. brown sugar/gula merah
60 ml. fish sauce
80 g. dried prawns (soaked &
  finely chopped)
2 red chillies
4-6 bird's eye ⎱ finely
  chillies/cili padi ⎰ chopped
4 shallots
1 tablespoon dried shrimp paste/
  belacan (roasted)
1-2 tablespoons lime juice

1 **To prepare dip:** Combine brown sugar and fish sauce in a small pot.

2 Cook over low heat till boiling. Reduce heat and simmer.

3 When the sauce is quite thick, add in dried prawns, red chillies, *cili padi* and dried shrimp paste.

4 Simmer till thickened and add lime juice to taste. Add in salt, if necessary.

5 Put in chopped shallots and remove from heat.

6 Leave to cool before serving with the assorted vegetables.

TIPS

Increase the amount of *cili padi* if you prefer.

FISH HEAD MEEHOON SOUP

Serves 4

1 threadfin/senangin fish head
1 *l* chicken stock
6 slices ginger
100 g. salted vegetables
1 tomato (cut into wedges)
some *tung choy*
300 g. rice noodles/meehoon
   (soaked and drained)
3 stalks mustard greens/sawi
   (scalded, drained and cut
   lengthwise)
oil for frying

MARINADE INGREDIENTS
1 tablespoon chilli powder
1 tablespoon cornflour

SEASONING INGREDIENTS
1 tablespoon chicken stock
   granules
1 teaspoon ground pepper

1 Clean fish head and cut into 4 portions. Pat fish dry with a cloth. Marinade fish with marinade ingredients. Put aside.

2 Heat oil and fry the fish head until golden brown. Remove and drain.

3 Bring the chicken stock to the boil with the fish head, sliced ginger, salted vegetables, tomato wedges, *tung choy* and seasoning ingredients. Boil for 20 minutes. **Remove from stove.**

4 Arrange the *meehoon* and mustard greens in a serving bowl. Ladle the soup on top of *meehoon*. Serve hot.

CHAOZHOU STEAMED FISH

Serves 4

650 g. siakap fish fillet (gutted &
scored)
200 g. chicken meat (gutted &
scored)
100 g. ginger slices
100 g. salted vegetables (finely
sliced)
1 red chilli (thinly sliced)
2 stalks coriander leaves (cut
lengthwise)
2 dried mushrooms (soaked and
thinly sliced)
1 tomato (thinly sliced)
1 cake bean curd (thinly sliced)

SEASONING INGREDIENTS
a dash of sesame oil
a pinch of salt
1 teaspoon chicken stock
granules
1 teaspoon fried shallots oil
2 sour plums (crushed)

1 Place fish in the centre of
serving dish.

2 Arrange the shredded
chicken, ginger slices, salted
vegetables and coriander leaves
on the fish. Then arrange the
mushrooms, tomato and
beancurd around the fish.

3 Combine the seasoning
ingredients and mix well. Pour
onto the fish and steam for
10-15 minutes.

4 Remove fish and serve hot.

MURTABAK

Serves 4-6

PANCAKE INGREDIENTS
600 g. all-purpose flour
½ teaspoon salt
sufficient water
80 g. ghee

FILLING INGREDIENTS
2 tablespoons oil
2 large onions (finely chopped)
400 g. minced chicken/beef
1 tablespoon meat curry powder
½ teaspoon black pepper powder
salt to taste
5-6 eggs (beaten)

SAUCE INGREDIENTS
1 large onion (finely
  sliced)
3-4 tablespoons   } well-
  vinegar   } mixed
a pinch of sugar
a dash of red colouring

3 **To prepare dough:** Mix flour, salt and ghee. Add in water, a little at a time, and bind the ingredients into a dough. Knead dough for 10 minutes or till it is soft and pliable. Shape dough into 6-7 balls; rub a little ghee on each ball. Set aside for 2-3 hours.

6 Mix the egg with the minced meat.

1 Heat oil; sauté chopped onions till fragrant. Put in minced meat; stir till dry.

4 Flatten a ball of dough with the palm of your hand.

7 Place the flattened dough piece on a flat pan. Spoon some filling in the middle of the dough.

2 Add in meat curry powder, black pepper powder and salt. Stir till fragrant.

5 Slowly pull the sides of the dough till it becomes a large circular piece.

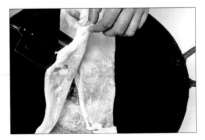

8 Fold into a neat rectangle. Fry till golden brown, then remove.

ASSAM LAKSA

Serves 4

2 l water
1 medium-sized *ikan sepat* (gutted and drained)
100 g. dried assam slices/asam gelugur (washed)
100 g. polygonum leaves/daun kesum (washed and leaves plucked)
100 g. galangal/lengkuas ⎫
1 stalk lemon grass/ ⎬ bruised
serai ⎭
1 ginger plant bud/bunga kantan (halved)
3 teaspoons prawn paste
2 teaspoons seasoning powder
salt to taste
1 kg. *laksa* noodles (scalded and drained)

GARNISHING INGREDIENTS
1 slice pineapple (thinly sliced)
1 cucumber (sliced thinly and lengthwise)
2 red chillies ⎫
1 large onion ⎬ thinly sliced
6 stalks mint leaves/daun pudina (plucked and washed)

1 Boil the *ikan sepat* in water. When cooked, remove fish and debone. Flake the meat and set aside.

2 Strain the water. Add in the flaked fish, assam slices, polygonum leaves, galangal, lemon grass and ginger flower. Leave to simmer slowly until well-cooked.

3 Add prawn paste, seasoning powder and salt. Let it remain hot.

4 Place *laksa* noodles in bowls and ladle the hot soup over noodles. Sprinkle with pineapple slices, cucumber slices, sliced red chillies, onion slices and mint leaves.

5 Serve *assam laksa* hot.

DODOL

Serves 10-12

6 coconuts (grated)
water (to squeeze coconut)
900 g. glutinous rice flour/
tepung pulut
150 g. rice flour
1.8 kg. palm sugar/gula
melaka
750 ml. water
3 screwpine/pandan leaves
(knotted)

1 Squeeze coconuts with water to yield 2 litres of thick milk. Set aside.

2 Squeeze again to obtain sufficient thin coconut milk.

3 Combine glutinous rice flour and rice flour with the thin coconut milk.

4 Strain mixture into a large wok.

5 Bring to the boil palm sugar, 750 ml. water and *pandan* leaves till the sugar dissolves.

6 Strain sugar syrup onto flour mixture.

7 Stir well over low heat till mixture is half-cooked.

8 Gradually pour in the thick coconut milk. Keep on stirring the mixture till it is very thick, oily and dark brown in colour. If *dodol* does not stick to the fingers, it is cooked.

9 Transfer *dodol* to a container lined with banana leaves. Serve.

CHINESE RADISH CAKE

Serves 4

500 g. **Chinese radish (peeled
 and cut into thin strips)**
500 g. **rice flour**
100 g. *Tang* **flour**
200 g. **dried shrimp granules**
600 ml. **cold water**
1 *l* **boiling water**
oil for frying

SEASONING INGREDIENTS
2 **tablespoons oil**
1 **tablespoon chicken stock
 granules**
1 **tablespoon chilli powder**
½ **teaspoon five spice powder**
salt to taste

1 Heat 2 tablespoonfuls oil; fry
Chinese radish with the
seasoning ingredients until well-
combined. Remove and put
aside.

2 Put rice flour, *Tang* flour and
dried shrimp granules in a
mixing bowl. Gradually pour in
cold water while stirring it. Beat
mixture to get rid of lumps.

3 Pour in boiling water; beat
until mixture is half-cooked.
Add in the fried Chinese radish
and stir well.

4 Pour the mixture into a
steamer tray. Steam for
30 minutes. When cooked,
remove and leave mixture to
cool in the tray for one night.

5 Remove the cake from the
tray. Cut to medium-sized
shapes.

6 Heat oil; fry the cakes over
moderate heat until golden
brown. Remove and drain well.

7 Serve hot with chilli sauce.

RENDANG AYAM

Serves 4-6

1 chicken (cut into 12 pieces)
½ grated coconut
100 ml. oil
8 shallots (thinly sliced)
5 cm. cinnamon stick ⎫ dry
4 star anise   ⎬ spices
6 cardamoms   ⎭
1.2 l coconut milk (from 1½ coconuts)
1 slice dried assam
4 turmeric leaves/daun kunyit (finely shredded)
4 daun limau purut/lime leaves
salt & sugar to taste

BLENDED INGREDIENTS
3 large onions
5 cloves garlic
3 stalks lemon grass/serai
2.5 cm. ginger
2.5 cm. turmeric/kunyit
2.5 cm. galangal/lengkuas
15-20 dried chillies (soaked till soft)

1 Dry-fry grated coconut till golden brown. Pound or blend to make *kerisik*.

2 Heat oil and fry shallots till crispy. Put in a food processor with the blended ingredients and process till fine.

3 Re-heat oil and sauté dry spices for 1 minute.

4 Add in blended paste; stir till the oil separates.

5 Combine chicken pieces, coconut milk and dried assam.

6 Cook till boiling and gravy is reduced by half. Add *kerisik*.

7 Mix turmeric leaves and *daun limau purut* thoroughly. Season to taste.

8 Continue cooking till the gravy is very thick. Serve with boiled white rice or *ketupat*.

KETAM MASAK PEDAS *(Hot and Spicy Crabs)*

Serves 4

1 kg. crabs (any variety)
200 g. dried shrimps (soaked and drained)
10 bird's eye chillies/cili padi (crushed)
1 teaspoon chopped garlic
1 teaspoon chopped large onion
a few curry leaves/daun kari
1 teaspoon seafood curry powder
2 tablespoons oyster sauce
1 tablespoon sour plum sauce
oil for sautéing

1 Clean the crabs and halve them. Discard the outer hard shells and clean the insides. Cut crabs into medium-sized pieces. Discard thinner portions of the legs and smash the pincers. Put aside.

2 Heat some oil and fry dried shrimps over low heat until golden. Put aside.

3 Retain about 2 tablespoonfuls oil in the wok. Sauté bird's eye chillies, garlic, onions, curry leaves and seafood curry powder until fragrant.

4 Add in the crabs and fry over high heat for a short while. Reduce the heat, cover the wok and cook for a further 8-10 minutes or until the crab shells turn red in colour.

5 Put in the sour plum sauce, oyster sauce and fried dried shrimps. Mix well.

6 Dish out crabs onto a serving plate and serve hot.

AYAM MASAK KICAP *(Chicken with Soya Sauce)*

Serves 4-6

1 chicken (cut into 10 pieces)
½ teaspoon turmeric powder/
serbuk kunyit
salt to taste
oil for frying
4 cm. cinnamon stick
2 star anise
2 tablespoons oyster sauce
2 tablespoons tomato
sauce
4 tablespoons sweet soya } **mixed**
sauce
1 teaspoon thick soya
sauce
a little water
1 large onion (sliced into rings)
2 red chillies } **halved**
2 green chillies
sugar to taste

BLENDED INGREDIENTS
5 shallots
3 cloves garlic
1 cm. ginger

1 Marinate chicken pieces with turmeric powder and salt for 30 minutes.

2 Deep-fry chicken pieces in hot oil till cooked through.

3 Remove all but 3 tablespoons oil. Sauté cinnamon stick and star anise for 1 minute.

4 Stir in blended ingredients. Fry till aromatic.

5 Then pour in mixed sauces and some water; stir till sauce is boiling.

6 Put in chicken pieces and stir for 3 minutes.

7 Mix in onion rings, red and green chillies.

8 Season to taste with sugar. Dish up and serve.

MIXED TOM YAM

Serves 6

200 g. squids — cut into
100 g. fish fillet — bite-sized
200 g. *siput lala* — pieces
200 g. medium-sized prawns (deveined)
3 shallots (finely minced)
2 stalks lemon grass/serai (cut 5 cm. & bruised)
2.5 cm. galangal/lengkuas (thinly sliced)
750 ml. water
2 tablespoons fish sauce
5 lime leaves/daun limau purut
2 tomatoes (quartered)
4-5 bird's eye chillies/cili padi (bruised)
1 teaspoon chilli paste
3 tablespoons lime juice
4 sprigs coriander leaves — finely
4 stalks spring onion — chopped
salt & sugar to taste

1 Combine shallots, lemon grass, galangal and water; bring to the boil.

2 Add the squids, fish, *siput lala*, prawns, fish sauce and lime leaves.

3 Stir and cook till boiling. Season with salt and sugar.

4 Remove pot from heat; mix in tomatoes, bird's eye chillies, chilli paste and lime juice.

5 Dish up into bowls. Serve *tom yam*, sprinkled with chopped coriander leaves and spring onions.

PINDANG SERANI

Serves 3-4

500 g. threadfin/ikan senangin
(sliced into pieces)
2 tablespoons oil
1 stalk lemon grass/serai (bruised)
750 ml. water
10 small sour starfruits/belimbing
buluh
1-2 teaspoons lime juice
salt & sugar to taste

BLENDED INGREDIENTS
5 shallots
2 cloves garlic
3 red chillies
1 cm. turmeric/kunyit
½ cm. galangal/lengkuas

1 Sauté blended ingredients and lemon grass in hot oil till aromatic.

2 Mix in water, salt and sugar.

3 Bring to the boil; put in the fish pieces and starfruits.

4 Simmer till the fish pieces are well-cooked. Adjust seasoning to taste.

5 Add lime juice; mix well with the fish pieces.

6 Remove from heat and serve hot with boiled white rice.

STUFFED BEAN CURD

Serves 4

8 cakes bean curd
½ teaspoon turmeric powder/
   serbuk kunyit
½ teaspoon salt
oil for frying
1 medium cucumber (tender part
   discarded & julienned)
200 g. bean sprouts (tailed &
   blanched)

SAUCE INGREDIENTS
40 g. granulated sugar
50 ml. vinegar
salt to taste ⎱ finely
3 red chillies ⎰ chopped
   (seeded)
2 cloves garlic
3 tablespoons fried & skinned
   groundnuts (finely chopped)
2 tablespoons toasted sesame
   seeds

1 Cut the bean curd diagonally into two pieces. Make a slit along the opening; do not cut through bean curd.

2 Rub bean curd with turmeric powder and salt.

3 Heat oil in a wok; deep-fry bean curd till golden. Remove from heat and drain well on paper towel.

4 Combine cucumber and bean sprouts. Stuff into the bean curd opening. (the insides may be spooned out to make room for more stuffing). Arrange bean curd on a serving platter.

5 **To prepare sauce:** Bring to the boil sugar, vinegar and salt over low heat. When mixture thickens, remove from heat and keep warm. Mix in chopped chillies and garlic. Sprinkle with chopped groundnuts and toasted sesame seeds.

6 Serve sauce with the stuffed bean curd.

YONG TOW FOO

Serves 4

5 cakes bean curd
1 bitter gourd
1 brinjal
5 ladies' fingers
300 g soya beans (soaked & drained)
400 ml water
oil for frying

FILLING INGREDIENTS
500 g. Spanish mackerel/ tenggiri meat } finely chopped
200 g. chicken meat
200 g. prawns (shelled, deveined & coarsely chopped)
100 g. salted fish } soaked and chopped
100 g. dried *kapis*
3 dried black mushrooms
2 water chestnuts (peeled and chopped)
1 egg
a dash of pepper
a pinch of salt

SAUCE INGREDIENTS
200 ml. soya bean milk
1 teaspoon chopped garlic
1 tablespoon Hoisin sauce
1 tablespoon oil

1 Cut bean curd into half diagonally. Cut bitter gourd into 2-3 cm. lengths; discard the seeds. Cut brinjals at a slant with a 2-3 cm. thickness. Score the middle with a slanting cut. Slit ladies' fingers lengthwise; discard the seeds. Keep aside.

2 To prepare filling: Mix all the filling ingredients, sprinkling water occasionally while mixing. Knead until it is properly mixed. Beat the dough against a chopping board until mixture becomes pliable. Put aside.

3 Slit the middle of the bean curd with the point of a sharp knife and remove a small amount of bean curd from the centre. Fill in the space with the filling mixture until well-packed. Neaten using some water.

4 Repeat the process with the bitter gourd, brinjal and ladies' fingers. Leave aside.

5 Heat oil and fry the *yong tow foo* over low heat until cooked on both sides. Set aside.

6 Fry the soya beans without oil until fragrant. Add water and simmer for 20 minutes until soya beans are tender. Add in the fried *yong tow foo* and cook covered for 10 minutes. Dish out *yong tow foo* into a serving bowl.

7 To prepare sauce: Heat oil and sauté garlic till brown. Add in the rest of the sauce ingredients and simmer. Serve sauce separately with the *yong tow foo*.

CENCALUK-FLAVOURED CHICKEN

Serves 4

400 g. chicken breast
a pinch of cornflour
100 g. salted fish (soaked and
  drained)
3 bird's eye chillies/cili padi
  (crushed)
1 tablespoon ginger ⎱ chopped
1 tablespoon garlic ⎰
1 tablespoon *cencaluk*
3 tablespoons oil
some spring onions (chopped)

SEASONING INGREDIENTS
1 tablespoon oyster sauce
1 teaspoon sour plum sauce

1 Wash chicken and pat dry with a cloth. Cut into several pieces. Coat chicken with cornflour. Leave for 15 minutes.

2 Heat oil; fry the salted fish until golden. Add in the bird's eye chillies, chopped ginger and garlic. Sauté until fragrant. Reduce heat.

3 Add in chicken pieces and *cencaluk*. Stir-fry until well-mixed. Cover and cook for 10 minutes.

4 Put in the seasoning ingredients and increase the heat. Stir-fry well.

5 Remove when cooked. Sprinkle with chopped spring onions and serve hot.

YAM CAKE

Serves 4

1 medium-sized yam (peeled
  and diced small)
500 g rice flour
1 *l* cold water
1 *l* boiling water
oil for frying

SEASONING INGREDIENTS
1 tablespoon seasoning
  powder
1 teaspoon chilli powder
1 teaspoon five spice powder
a pinch of salt

GARNISHING INGREDIENTS
400 g. dried shrimps (soaked
  & drained)
200 g. *choy poh* (soaked and
  coarsely chopped)
some garlic (chopped)
some fried shallots
several stalks
  spring onions } chopped
3 tablespoons oil

1 Heat oil and fry the diced yam for 5-8 minutes. Remove and drain well.

2 Leave 2 tablespoonfuls oil in the wok. Heat oil; add in the seasoning ingredients and fried yam. Fry until well-mixed. Remove and keep aside.

3 Place the rice flour in a mixing bowl. Gradually, stir in the cold water into the bowl. Beat the mixture to discard lumps.

4 Pour boiling water into the mixture. Mix thoroughly until it becomes half-cooked. Add in the fried yam and stir until well-combined.

5 Pour mixture into a steamer tray. Steam for about 30 minutes. When cooked, remove and put aside.

6 Heat 3 tablespoonfuls oil. Sauté the dried shrimps, *choy poh* and chopped garlic until fragrant. Remove from heat.

7 Sprinkle fried shrimps, *choy poh* and garlic on the cooked yam, together with the fried shallots and spring onions.

8 Cut yam cake to preferred sizes and serve with chilli sauce.

FRIED FOUR ANGLED-BEANS

Serves 4

300 g. four angled-beans
  (sliced at a slant)
3 tablespoons oil
4 shallots
2 cloves garlic
2 red chillies
1 cm. dried shrimp } **blended/**
  paste/belacan **pounded**
4-6 bird's eye
  chillies/*cili padi*
40 g. dried anchovies (cleaned)
3 tablespoons oyster sauce
2 tablespoons chilli sauce
a little water
1 large onion (cut into
  wedges)
salt & sugar to taste

1 Sauté blended paste in hot oil till fragrant.

2 Add in dried anchovies, oyster sauce, chilli sauce and some water.

3 Stir till the gravy boils, then add in the four angled-beans.

4 Mix thoroughly and cover with a lid.

5 When the beans are tender, add onions, salt and sugar to taste.

6 Stir well and remove from heat. Serve.

POPIA (*Spring Rolls*)

Serves 6

2 tablespoons oil
4 red chillies
4 cloves garlic ⎫ blended
30 g. dried shrimps
 (soaked)
2 tablespoons oyster sauce
1 tablespoon thin soya sauce
200 g. prawns (shelled &
 minced)
200 g. bean sprouts (tailed)
5 shallots (finely sliced & fried
 crisp)
15-20 spring roll skin
oil for deep-frying
salt & sugar to taste
2 tablespoons all-purpose
 flour (mixed with water to a
 paste)

**FINELY SHREDDED
INGREDIENTS**
150 g. carrot
180 g. yam bean/sengkuang
150 g. cucumber (tender part
 discarded)

1 Heat the oil; sauté blended paste till fragrant.

2 Add oyster sauce, soya sauce and minced prawns. Stir till prawns are cooked.

3 Put in shredded carrot; mix for 3-4 minutes.

4 Combine yam bean, cucumber, bean sprouts, sugar and salt. When the vegetables are quite soft, remove from heat and allow to cool.

5 Place a spring roll skin on a wooden board. Spoon a little filling in a neat bar onto the skin. Sprinkle some fried shallots. Lift up one edge of skin to cover the filling.

6 Fold both ends of skin over to prevent filling from spilling out of the roll. Roll up skin and seal edges with some flour paste.

7 Deep-fry spring rolls in hot oil till crispy and golden brown. Drain oil.

8 Transfer to a serving plate. Serve spring rolls with chilli sauce, if desired.

MURUKU

Serves 6-8

3 eggs (lightly beaten)
600 g. dhal flour
250-300 ml. water } mixed
1 teaspoon salt
240 g. rice flour
1 tablespoon fennel powder
1 tablespoon cummin powder
160 g. margarine
oil for deep-frying
3-4 stalks curry leaves/daun kari

2 Add beaten egg and stir till even.

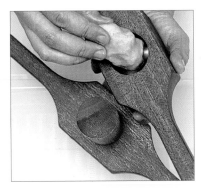

5 Place a portion of the dough into a *muruku* mould.

1 Mix dhal flour with salted water till well-combined.

3 Put in rice flour, fennel and cummin powder.

6 Heat oil for deep-frying. Press the handles of the mould in a circular motion over the hot oil.

4 Add margarine and continue kneading till a soft dough is obtained.

7 Fry with a few curry leaves till the *muruku* turns golden. Remove and drain on a paper towel. Cool *muruku* and then store in an airtight container.

KUIH TEPUNG PELITA

Serves 6-8

200 g. all-purpose flour
400 ml. thin coconut milk
** (from 1 coconut)**
8 screwpine/ } **blended &**
pandan leaves } **strained**
150 ml. water
a dash of green colouring
½ teaspoon salt
100 g. granulated sugar
180 ml. thick coconut milk
** (from 1 coconut)**
1 tablespoon rice flour
10 banana leaves (shaped into
** a *temalung* or basket)**
20 lidi sticks/stapler

1 Fold ends of banana leaves and secure with stapler. Fold the other end and secure again, forming a basket-shaped container or *temalung*.

2 Mix well flour, thin coconut milk, *pandan* juice, green colouring and salt till a smooth batter is obtained.

3 Spoon a little sugar into the *temalung*. Gradually, pour in the green batter till three-quarters full.

4 Steam *kuih* for 10 minutes or till set. Meanwhile, stir thick coconut milk and rice flour.

5 Pour the white batter carefully onto the set green portion.

6 Return to steamer and cook for 5 minutes. Remove from steamer; allow to cool before serving *kuih*.

PURI

Serves 4

200 g. plain flour
30 g. margarine
½ teaspoon salt
60 ml. warm water
70 ml. warm fresh milk
oil for deep-frying

1 Mix well flour, margarine and salt.

2 Add water and milk a little at a time; combine to form a soft dough.

3 Knead dough for 10-12 minutes; rub some oil on the surface of dough.

4 Cover dough with a clean tea towel. Set aside for 30 minutes.

5 Knead again and divide dough into small balls about 4 cm. in diameter.

6 On a floured surface, roll each ball into a 10 cm. circle.

7 Heat a lot of oil for deep-frying. Drop the *puri* one or two at a time into the hot oil.

8 Once the *puri* puffs up, turn them over. Fry for minute.

9 Remove from wok; drain well on a paper towel. Serve hot with curry.

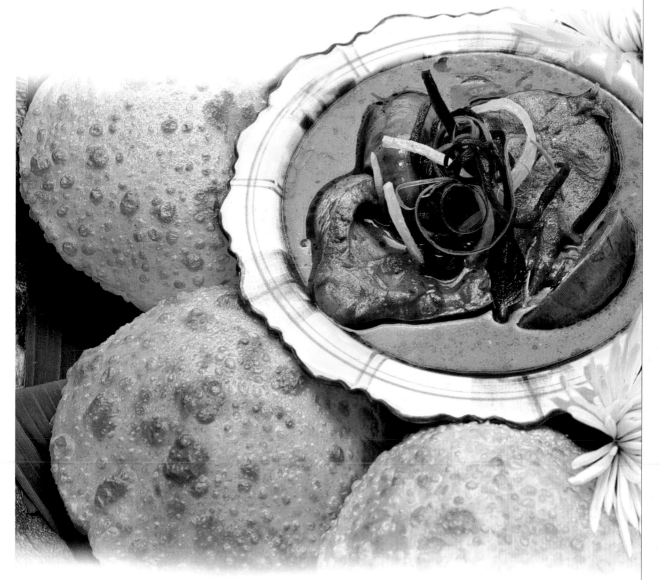

JALA EMAS

Serves 6-8

10 duck egg yolks
1 teaspoon rice flour
600 ml. water
210 g. granulated sugar
2 screwpine/pandan leaves
  (knotted)
40g. roasted cashew nuts
some red cherries

2 Strain egg mixture through a muslin cloth.

5 Put egg yolk in a triangular shaped plastic.

1 Beat egg yolks and rice flour till well-combined.

3 Squeeze the egg mixture into a bowl.

6 Drop the egg yolk in a circular motion into the boiling syrup.

4 Bring to the boil water, sugar and *pandan* leaves. When syrup is quite thick, discard *pandan* leaves.

7 Use 2 cocktail sticks/*lidi* to remove the *jala emas* from the syrup. Repeat the process till all the egg yolk is used up.

TIPS
If it is difficult to obtain duck eggs, use half chicken eggs and half duck eggs. Chicken eggs may be used exclusively, but the result will not be completely satisfactory.

LALA MASAK PEDAS *(Hot and Spicy Clams)*

Serves 4

1 kg. clams/lala
200 g. young ginger ⎫
100 g. red chillies ⎬ chopped
100 g. garlic ⎪
100 g. shallots ⎭
2 teaspoons Thai chilli sauce
2 tablespoons oyster sauce
a pinch of salt
a dash of vinegar
3 tablespoons oil

1 Add salt and a few drops of vinegar into a pot of water. Soak the clams in water to remove the mud inside the clams. Wash the clams, remove and drain well.

2 Heat the oil. Sauté the chopped ginger, red chillies, garlic and shallots until fragrant.

3 Add in the clams and cook over high heat for 15 minutes. Add in the Thai chilli sauce and oyster sauce. Fry until the sauce thickens.

4 Dish out onto a serving plate and serve clams hot.

KUIH ANG KOO

Serves 4

**500 g. glutinous rice flour/
  tepung pulut
sufficient water
a dash of red food colouring
oil to grease mould**

FILLING INGREDIENTS
**1 kg. peeled green beans
  (soaked until softened)
250 ml. water
2 screwpine/pandan leaves
800 g. castor sugar**

1 In a mixing bowl, mix 300 g. glutinous rice flour with sufficient water. Mix well. Knead to form a soft dough. Put into a steamer tray and steam for 5-10 minutes or until dough is cooked.

2 Remove from tray; add the remaining glutinous rice flour and red colouring. Knead until well-mixed. Put aside.

3 Put the soaked green beans into a steamer tray and steam until cooked. Pound until fine and set aside.

4 **To prepare filling:** Heat 250 ml water in a wok. Add in screwpine leaves and sugar. Simmer until sugar dissolves. Discard screwpine leaves and add in green bean. Stir until filling is thick and dry. Remove and leave to cool.

5 Prepare the mould by brushing it with oil. Set aside.

6 Pinch some dough and roll out to form a round shape. Put 1 tablespoonful filling and seal the edges. Press into the mould and take it out. Repeat process till all dough is used up.

7 Arrange the finished *ang koo* in a steamer tray. Steam for 15 minutes.

8 When cooked, remove from the steamer. Serve when cool.

BUTTERED-FLAVOURED PRAWNS

Serves 4

600 g. large prawns
oil for frying
3 tablespoons fresh milk
3 egg yolks
2 tablespoons margarine/
** butter**
1 tablespoons chopped garlic
6 bird's eye chillies/cili padi
** (crushed)**
a few curry leaves/daun kari

MARINADE INGREDIENTS
1 egg yolk
1 tablespoon rice flour

1 Wash prawns and drain. Cut the feelers but do not discard skins and tails. Make a long slit along the back of the prawns and discard the veins. Dry wtih a paper towel.

2 Mix the marinade ingredients and stir until well-combined. Add in prawns and mix thoroughly. Set aside for 15-20 minutes.

3 Heat oil. Fry prawns till brown. Remove and drain.

4 Pour milk and egg yolks into a bowl. Mix till smooth.

5 Melt the margarine in a wok. Gradually pour in the egg mixture. Fry over low heat and continue stirring to scramble the eggs.

6 Add in the prawns, chopped garlic, bird's eye chillies and curry leaves. Sauté over high heat until evenly cooked.

7 Remove from heat and serve immediately.

INDEX

A

Acar Sayur Campur 109
Ang Koo, Kuih 173
Asparagus with Prawns 72
Assam Laksa 152
Ayam Golek 26
Ayam Kurma 33
Ayam Masak Kicap 157
Ayam Masak Merah 102
Ayam Percik 115

B

Bahulu, Kuih 28
Beef Curry 18
Bergedel Daging 35
Bergedel Sayur 88
Bhujia Ladies' Fingers 21
Braised Chicken with Mushrooms 108
Buah Melaka 122
Bubur Cha Cha 87
Bubur Kacang Hijau 100
Buttered-Flavoured Prawns 174

C

Cencaluk-Flavoured Chicken 162
Cendol 29
Chang Parcels 95
Chaozhou Steamed Fish 149
Chapati 73
Chicken Kampung-Style 134
Chicken Kut Teh 145
Chicken Satay 116
Chicken Siew Pau 110
Chicken with Young Ginger 126
Chinese Radish Cake 154
Claypot Rice 24
Curry Mee 99
Curry Puffs 128

D

Daging Bakar Cecah Air Asam 80
Daging Masak Merah Ala Thai 34
Dendeng Daging 138
Dhal Curry 49
Dodol 153
Dry Chicken Curry 136

F

Fish Curry 51
Fish Head Curry 67
Fish Head Meehoon Soup 148
French Beans with Liver 71
Fried Choy Tam 50
Fried Cuttlefish with Mixed Vegetables 76
Fried Four Angled-Beans 164
Fried Kangkung with Belacan 141
Fried Lemon Chicken 16
Fried Pandan Chicken 89

G

Grilled Fish 121

H

Hailam Chicken Rice 39

I

Ice Cream Pudding 92
Ikan Pari Masak Asam Pedas 124
Ikan Patin Masak Tempoyak 56
Indian Fried Mee 53

J

Jala Emas 170
Johor Laksa 25

K

Kai Lan with Beef 37
Kambing Keema 46
Kerabu Pucuk Paku 63
Kerabu Tauge 81
Ketam Asam Pedas 15
Ketam Masak Lemak Cili Padi 82
Ketam Masak Pedas 156
Ketayap, Kuih 54
Ketupat 135
Koci, Kuih 74
Kole Kacang, Kuih 104
Kosui, Kuih 84
Kubis Masak Lemak 140

L

Laksam 114
Lala Masak Pedas 172
Lapis, Kuih 103
Lemang 98
Leng Chee Kang 131
Lepat Pisang 55
Loh Hon Kor 57
Lontong 113

M

Malay-Style Rojak 120
Maltose Chicken Wings 17
Masala Machi 133
Masala Vadei 130
Mee Bandung 101
Mee Jawa 69
Mee Siam 52
Mixed Fried Sambal 93
Mixed Tom Yam 158
Murtabak 150
Muruku 166
Mutton Kurma 19
Mutton Soup 129

N

Nasi Beriani Hujan Panas 70
Nasi Dagang – Gulai Ikan Tongkol 112
Nasi Kerabu 83
Nasi Lemak with Anchovy Sambal 77
Nasi Minyak 38
Nasi Ulam 137
Nyonya Fried Rice 64

O

Opor Ayam 44
Otak-otak 58

P

Paceri Nanas 48
Pakoras 132
Pecal 36
Penang Fried Kuey Teow 144
Pengat Pisang 111
Pindang Serani 159
Popia 165
Prawn Mee 96
Prawn Sambal with Petai 30
Pucuk Ubi Masak Tempoyak 125
Pulut Inti 143
Pulut Kuning 62
Puri 169
Putu Mayam 142

R

Rendang Ayam 155
Rendang Tok 139
Roti Canai 117

S

Samosas 40
Sayur Cekur Berkeledek 146
Seaweed Jelly 86
Seri Muka, Kuih 85
Serunding Ayam 79
Serunding Daging 42
Soto Ayam 32
Spicy Fried Chicken 23
Spicy Fried Prawns 47
Spicy Fried Squids 68
Squids in Spicy Santan 94
Stir-fried Mixed Vegetables 20
Stuffed Bean curd 160
Stuffed Fried Cencaru 119
Stuffed Squids 106
Sup Tulang 43
Sweet and Sour Fish 31
Sweet and Sour Fish Soup 65
Szechuan Tofu 118

T

Talam, Kuih 60
Tandoori Chicken 66
Tau Foo Fa 61
Telur Bungkus Daging 90
Tepung Pelita, Kuih 168
Thosai 105
Tomato Rice 22

U

Ulam dengan Cicah 147

Y

Yam Cake 163
Yam in Assam Gravy 127
Yang Zhou Fried Rice 78
Yau Cha Kwai 45
Yong Tow Foo 161

V

Vegetable Soup 97

OTHER LARGE FORMAT COOKBOOKS (19 cm × 26.5 cm)

FESTIVE DELIGHTS

Yummy CAKES

Tasty COOKIES & BISCUITS

Halal CHINESE COOKING (for MALAYSIA & SINGAPORE)

Delicious FAMILY RECIPES

Delightful ASEAN CUISINE

TEMPTING Local Desserts

Crunchy & Crispy BISCUITS

Fine & Tasty CAKES

ALL TESTED recipes   Every recipe illustrated

Best of FOOD COURT DISHES

ALL TESTED recipes   Every recipe illustrated

Delicious LOCAL CAKES & KUIH

OTHER TITLES UNDER PUBLICATION

- Best of Food Court Dishes
- Delicious Local Cakes & Kuih
- Quick & Easy Home Meals & Snacks
- Popular Hawker Delights
- Hot & Spicy Dishes
- Traditional Malaysian Flavours

OTHER SMALL FORMAT COOKBOOKS (13 cm × 19 cm)

Malaysian HI-TEA DELIGHTS

TEA-TIME CAKES & COOKIES

Better BISCUITS CAKES & DESSERTS

Special CAKES & BISCUITS

Traditional Malay KUIH

Light Meals & SNACKS

EASY-TO-COOK MEALS

Favourite MALAYSIAN CUISINE

Tasty & Healthy COOKING

FISH AND CHICKEN DISHES

Everyday MALAYSIAN RECIPES

MALAY HOME COOKING